Kinky Cosmos

Kinky Cosmos

Matthew Petchinsky

publisher logo

Kinky Cosmos: Sexual Kink Astrology for Every Sign
By: Matthew Petchinsky

Introduction

Welcome and Explanation of the Book's Concept

Welcome to "Kinky Cosmos: Sexual Kink Astrology for Every Sign." This book is a unique fusion of two fascinating realms: astrology and sexual exploration. Our journey together will delve into how the celestial bodies influence our deepest desires, fantasies, and sexual preferences. By understanding the cosmic energies that shape our personalities and drives, you can unlock new dimensions of pleasure and intimacy in your relationships.

Astrology has long been a tool for self-discovery, helping individuals understand their traits, motivations, and behaviors. In this book, we extend this understanding to the bedroom, offering insights into how your zodiac sign and the movements of celestial bodies can affect your sexual inclinations and experiences. Whether you're an astrology enthusiast or a curious newcomer, this guide will provide you with valuable knowledge to enhance your sexual journey.

Brief Overview of Astrology, Cosmic Events, Moon Phases, Planetary Alignments, and the Wiccan Wheel of the Year

Astrology

Astrology is the study of how the positions and movements of celestial bodies—such as the sun, moon, planets, and stars—affect human life. Each zodiac sign, corresponding to different times of the year, is associated with specific traits and tendencies. By examining these signs and their ruling planets, astrologers can provide insights into various aspects of life, including personality, relationships, and sexuality.

Cosmic Events

Cosmic events, such as eclipses, retrogrades, and transits, have profound impacts on our lives. These events are moments when the regular movements of celestial bodies interact in unique ways, creating powerful energetic shifts. For example, a solar eclipse might bring sudden changes and revelations, while a planetary retrograde could prompt reflection and reevaluation. Understanding these events can help you navigate their influences on your sexual desires and relationships.

Moon Phases

The moon, with its waxing and waning phases, has a significant impact on our emotions and behaviors. The lunar cycle consists of eight distinct phases: New Moon, Waxing Crescent, First Quarter, Waxing Gibbous, Full Moon, Waning Gibbous, Last Quarter, and Waning Crescent. Each phase carries its own energy and can influence our sexual appetites and moods. For instance, the Full Moon is often associated with heightened emotions and increased libido, while the New Moon signifies new beginnings and setting intentions.

Planetary Alignments

Planetary alignments occur when planets form specific angles with each other, known as aspects. These alignments can amplify or challenge the energies of the planets involved. Conjunctions, oppositions, trines, squares, and sextiles are some of the main aspects that shape astrological interpretations. These alignments can affect your sexual energy, attraction to others, and the dynamics within your intimate relationships. By understanding the current planetary alignments, you can better harness their influences to enhance your sexual experiences.

The Wiccan Wheel of the Year

The Wiccan Wheel of the Year is a calendar that marks eight festivals, known as Sabbats, celebrating the changing seasons and the cycle of nature. These Sabbats include Yule, Imbolc, Ostara, Beltane, Litha, Lammas, Mabon, and Samhain. Each festival has its own themes and energies, which can be aligned with sexual exploration and expression.

For example, Beltane, celebrated on May 1st, is a festival of fertility and passion, making it an ideal time to explore new sexual adventures.

How These Elements Influence Sexual Kinks and Preferences

Our sexual kinks and preferences are deeply intertwined with the energies of the cosmos. Just as the planets influence our personalities, they also shape our sexual desires and fantasies. Each zodiac sign has its own sexual archetype, influenced by its ruling planet and element (fire, earth, air, water). By understanding your sign's sexual traits, you can gain insights into what turns you on and how to communicate your desires to your partner.

Cosmic events, moon phases, planetary alignments, and the Wiccan Wheel of the Year add additional layers of complexity to our sexual experiences. For instance, a Venus retrograde might prompt you to reassess your relationships and sexual needs, while a Full Moon could heighten your libido and bring your fantasies to the forefront. The seasonal festivals of the Wiccan Wheel provide opportunities to celebrate and honor your sexuality in harmony with the natural world.

Throughout this book, we will explore how these astrological and cosmic elements influence each zodiac sign's sexual kinks and preferences. By aligning yourself with the rhythms of the universe, you can deepen your understanding of your desires, enhance your sexual satisfaction, and cultivate more intimate and fulfilling relationships.

Prepare to embark on an enlightening journey through the stars and into the depths of your own sexual psyche. The cosmos holds the key to unlocking your true sexual potential—let's explore it together in "Kinky Cosmos: Sexual Kink Astrology for Every Sign."

Chapter 1: The Foundations of Sexual Kink Astrology
Introduction to Astrology and Its Connection to Sexuality and Kinks

Astrology, the ancient art of divining human destiny through the movements and positions of celestial bodies, offers profound insights into many aspects of our lives, including our sexuality. The stars and planets not only guide our personalities and life paths but also shape our deepest desires and fantasies. By understanding the connection between astrology and sexuality, you can gain valuable knowledge about your sexual kinks and preferences.

Each of the twelve zodiac signs, governed by different planets and elements, exhibits unique traits and tendencies. These astrological influences extend to our sexual behaviors and inclinations. For example, fiery Aries may have a bold and adventurous approach to sex, while sensual Taurus seeks comfort and pleasure in the physicality of their intimate encounters. By exploring these connections, you can better understand your sexual nature and how to fulfill your desires.

Astrology also takes into account the positions of the sun, moon, and planets at the time of your birth. This celestial snapshot, known as your natal chart or birth chart, serves as a map of your personality and potential. Within this chart lie clues to your sexual preferences, kinks, and the dynamics of your intimate relationships. By learning how to read and interpret your chart, you can uncover these hidden aspects of your sexual self.

How to Read Your Astrological Chart for Insights into Kinks and Preferences

Reading your astrological chart might seem daunting at first, but with a little guidance, you can unlock its secrets and gain a deeper understanding of your sexual nature. Your natal chart is a circular diagram divided into twelve sections, each representing a different area of life, called houses. The positions of the sun, moon, and planets within these houses provide insights into various aspects of your personality and experiences.

Key Components of the Natal Chart

1. **Sun Sign**
   - Represents your core identity and ego.
   - Provides general traits and tendencies, including sexual preferences.
   - Example: An Aquarius sun might seek unconventional and intellectual sexual experiences.

2. **Moon Sign**
   - Governs your emotional needs and instincts.
   - Influences your emotional approach to sex and intimacy.
   - Example: A Cancer moon may crave emotional connection and security in sexual relationships.

3. **Ascendant (Rising Sign)**
   - Reflects your outward behavior and first impressions.
   - Can indicate your initial sexual approach and attraction style.
   - Example: A Scorpio rising might come across as intense and magnetic in sexual encounters.

4. **Venus**
   - The planet of love, beauty, and pleasure.
   - Directly influences your romantic and sexual inclinations.
   - Example: Venus in Leo may enjoy grand romantic gestures and a bit of drama in the bedroom.

5. **Mars**
   - The planet of action, desire, and sexuality.
   - Governs your sexual drive and the way you pursue pleasure.
   - Example: Mars in Aries might indicate a bold, direct, and adventurous approach to sex.

Interpreting the Houses

Each house in your natal chart corresponds to different aspects of life. Some houses are particularly significant when exploring your sexual kinks and preferences:

1. **5th House** - The House of Pleasure
   - Rules romance, creativity, and sexual expression.
   - The planets in this house reveal your approach to fun, flirting, and erotic play.
   - Example: Jupiter in the 5th house may indicate a love for expansive, joyful, and adventurous sexual experiences.

2. **7th House** - The House of Partnerships
   - Governs long-term relationships and partnerships.
   - Provides insights into what you seek in a committed sexual relationship.
   - Example: Saturn in the 7th house might suggest a need for stability and commitment in sexual partnerships.

3. **8th House** - The House of Sex and Transformation
   - Directly relates to sex, intimacy, and shared resources.
   - Reveals your deeper sexual desires and transformative experiences.
   - Example: Pluto in the 8th house could indicate a fascination with power dynamics and intense sexual encounters.

Aspects and Their Influence

Aspects are the angles formed between planets in your natal chart. They indicate how the energies of different planets interact with each other. Key aspects to consider when exploring sexual kinks and preferences include:

1. **Conjunctions**
   - Planets close together, blending their energies.

- ◦ Example: A Venus-Mars conjunction might suggest a strong alignment between love and sexual desire.

2. **Trines and Sextiles**
   - ◦ Harmonious aspects that facilitate ease and flow.
   - ◦ Example: A Moon-Venus trine may indicate a natural ability to express affection and emotional intimacy.

3. **Squares and Oppositions**
   - ◦ Challenging aspects that create tension and growth.
   - ◦ Example: A Mars-Saturn square could suggest conflicts between sexual desire and self-discipline.

Practical Steps to Reading Your Chart

1. **Obtain Your Natal Chart**
   - ◦ You can generate your natal chart using online tools or consult an astrologer.
   - ◦ Ensure you have accurate birth data: date, time, and place of birth.

2. **Identify Key Placements**
   - ◦ Note the positions of your sun, moon, ascendant, Venus, and Mars.
   - ◦ Examine which houses these planets occupy and any significant aspects they form.

3. **Interpret the Influences**
   - ◦ Use the traits and themes associated with each placement to understand your sexual kinks and preferences.
   - ◦ Consider how the elements (fire, earth, air, water) and modalities (cardinal, fixed, mutable) of your signs influence your sexual expression.

4. **Synthesize the Information**
   - ◦ Combine insights from different placements to form a comprehensive picture of your sexual nature.

◦ Reflect on how these astrological influences resonate with your personal experiences and desires.

By exploring the foundations of sexual kink astrology, you can gain a deeper appreciation for the cosmic forces that shape your intimate life. This knowledge empowers you to embrace your sexual self with confidence and authenticity, opening the door to richer and more fulfilling sexual experiences. In the following chapters, we will delve into each zodiac sign and their unique sexual kinks, guided by the celestial wisdom that the stars have to offer.

Chapter 2: Aries - Bold and Dominant
Sexual Characteristics and Kinks of Aries

Aries, the first sign of the zodiac, is ruled by Mars, the planet of action, desire, and aggression. As a fire sign, Aries is known for its bold, passionate, and dominant nature. In the realm of sexuality, Aries is adventurous, assertive, and often takes the lead. Those born under this sign are driven by a strong desire for excitement and novelty, making their sexual encounters dynamic and thrilling.

Key Sexual Characteristics of Aries

1. **Adventurous Spirit**
   - Aries loves to explore and try new things in the bedroom.
   - They are always up for a challenge and seek to keep their sexual experiences fresh and exciting.
2. **Dominant Nature**
   - Aries enjoys being in control and often takes the lead in sexual encounters.
   - They are assertive and direct about their desires, ensuring that their needs are met.
3. **Passionate and Fiery**
   - This sign is known for its intense passion and high libido.
   - Their sexual energy is abundant, making them enthusiastic and eager lovers.
4. **Impulsive and Spontaneous**
   - Aries acts on impulse, which can lead to spontaneous and exhilarating sexual experiences.
   - They thrive on the thrill of the moment and are not afraid to take risks.

5. **Competitive Edge**
   ◦ Aries has a competitive streak, which can translate into a desire to impress and outperform in bed.
   ◦ They enjoy the challenge of winning over their partner and being the best lover.

Common Sexual Kinks of Aries

Aries' dominant and adventurous nature lends itself to various sexual kinks and preferences. Here are some common kinks associated with this fiery sign:

1. **Dominance and Submission**
   ◦ Aries often enjoys taking on the dominant role in a BDSM dynamic.
   ◦ They find pleasure in exerting control and guiding their partner through intense experiences.
2. **Role-Playing**
   ◦ This sign loves to step into different personas and scenarios to spice up their sexual encounters.
   ◦ Role-playing allows Aries to explore new dynamics and keep their experiences fresh.
3. **Rough Play**
   ◦ Aries is drawn to rough and physical forms of play, such as spanking, biting, and hair-pulling.
   ◦ These intense sensations align with their desire for excitement and adrenaline.
4. **Exhibitionism**
   ◦ The bold and confident nature of Aries can lead to a fascination with exhibitionism.
   ◦ They enjoy the thrill of being watched and showing off their sexual prowess.

5. **Adventure and Risk**
- ° Aries thrives on the excitement of trying new and daring activities, such as outdoor sex or sex in unconventional locations.
- ° Their love for adventure extends to their sexual experiences, pushing boundaries and exploring new territories.

Recommended Kinks and Practices for Aries

To fully satisfy an Aries lover, it's important to cater to their adventurous and dominant nature. Here are some recommended kinks and practices that can enhance their sexual experiences:

1. **Power Play**
- ° Engage in power play dynamics, where Aries can take on the dominant role.
- ° Use restraints, blindfolds, and commands to create a controlled and thrilling environment.

2. **Spontaneity**
- ° Keep the element of surprise alive by initiating spontaneous sexual encounters.
- ° Plan unexpected dates or adventures that lead to passionate and unplanned moments.

3. **Intense Foreplay**
- ° Aries enjoys foreplay that builds anticipation and excitement.
- ° Incorporate rough play, such as light spanking or biting, to heighten their arousal.

4. **Role-Playing Scenarios**
- ° Introduce various role-playing scenarios that allow Aries to explore different dynamics and fantasies.

- Create characters and settings that challenge their creativity and enhance their excitement.

5. **Outdoor and Public Encounters**
    - Aries' love for adventure can be satisfied by engaging in outdoor or semi-public sexual activities.
    - Choose secluded but thrilling locations to add an element of risk and excitement.

6. **Physical Challenges**
    - Incorporate physical challenges or games that cater to Aries' competitive nature.
    - Activities like strip poker, sex dice, or erotic dares can add fun and excitement to their experiences.

How Aries is Influenced by Moon Phases, Cosmic Events, and Planetary Alignments

The sexual energy of Aries can be further enhanced or influenced by the phases of the moon, cosmic events, and planetary alignments. Understanding these influences can help you align your sexual experiences with the cosmic rhythms.

Moon Phases

1. **New Moon**
    - The New Moon is a time for new beginnings and setting intentions.
    - Aries can use this phase to explore new sexual practices or initiate a fresh dynamic in their relationship.

2. **Waxing Crescent**
    - As the moon begins to grow, so does Aries' desire for adventure and experimentation.
    - This phase is ideal for planning new sexual escapades and trying out different kinks.

3. **First Quarter**
    ◦ The First Quarter Moon brings a surge of energy and determination.
    ◦ Aries can harness this energy to take charge in the bedroom and push their sexual boundaries.
4. **Waxing Gibbous**
    ◦ With the Full Moon approaching, Aries' sexual energy and excitement build.
    ◦ This is a great time for engaging in intense and passionate encounters.
5. **Full Moon**
    ◦ The Full Moon heightens emotions and sexual desires, making Aries even more passionate and adventurous.
    ◦ This phase is perfect for indulging in bold and daring sexual activities.
6. **Waning Gibbous**
    ◦ As the moon begins to wane, Aries can focus on reflecting and deepening their sexual connection.
    ◦ Use this time for intimate and meaningful experiences that strengthen the bond with their partner.
7. **Last Quarter**
    ◦ The Last Quarter Moon is a time for reassessment and letting go.
    ◦ Aries can release any sexual practices or dynamics that no longer serve them and explore new possibilities.
8. **Waning Crescent**
    ◦ This final phase before the New Moon is ideal for rest and rejuvenation.
    ◦ Aries can take this time to recharge their sexual energy and prepare for new adventures.

Cosmic Events

1. Solar Eclipses

- Solar Eclipses bring powerful shifts and transformations.
- Aries can harness this energy to initiate significant changes in their sexual relationships and explore new dynamics.

2. Lunar Eclipses

- Lunar Eclipses heighten emotions and reveal hidden desires.
- Aries can use this time to delve into their deepest fantasies and bring them to the surface.

3. Retrogrades

- When planets go retrograde, it's a time for reflection and reevaluation.
- Aries can revisit past sexual experiences, learn from them, and make necessary adjustments.

4. Transits

- Transits, when planets move through different signs, bring varying influences.
- Aries can align their sexual practices with these energies to enhance their experiences.

Planetary Alignments

1. Mars Transits

- As the ruling planet of Aries, Mars transits significantly impact their sexual energy.
- During positive transits, Aries will feel an increase in libido and assertiveness.

2. Venus Transits

- Venus influences love and pleasure, and its transits can enhance Aries' romantic and sexual experiences.

- Positive Venus transits bring harmony and passion to their relationships.

3. **Jupiter Transits**
   - Jupiter brings expansion and growth, which can translate to sexual exploration and adventure.
   - Aries may feel a desire to broaden their sexual horizons and try new things.

4. **Saturn Transits**
   - Saturn's influence can bring structure and discipline to Aries' sexual life.
   - This is a good time for setting boundaries and establishing healthy sexual practices.

By understanding the sexual characteristics, recommended practices, and cosmic influences of Aries, you can enhance your sexual experiences and deepen your intimate connections. Embrace the bold and dominant energy of Aries and let it guide you to new heights of pleasure and excitement.

Chapter 3: Taurus - Sensual and Submissive
Sexual Characteristics and Kinks of Taurus

Taurus, the second sign of the zodiac, is ruled by Venus, the planet of love, beauty, and sensuality. As an earth sign, Taurus is grounded, patient, and deeply connected to the physical world. This connection extends to their sexuality, where they prioritize touch, comfort, and a slow, indulgent approach to pleasure. Taurus lovers are known for their stamina, dedication, and a strong preference for sensual experiences.

Key Sexual Characteristics of Taurus

1. **Sensuality**
   - Taurus has a heightened appreciation for the senses, making them highly sensual lovers.
   - They enjoy engaging in activities that involve touch, taste, smell, sight, and sound, enhancing their sexual experiences.

2. **Submissive Nature**
   - While Taurus can be strong-willed in many areas of life, they often enjoy taking on a more submissive role in the bedroom.
   - They find pleasure in being cared for, guided, and sometimes dominated by their partner.

3. **Patience and Stamina**
   - Taurus is not in a hurry when it comes to sex; they prefer to take their time and savor each moment.
   - Their stamina allows them to engage in long, drawn-out sessions of lovemaking, ensuring that their partner feels fully satisfied.

4. Romantic and Affectionate

- ° Taurus is naturally romantic and enjoys expressing affection through physical touch and gestures.
- ° They often seek a deep emotional connection with their partner, making their sexual experiences more meaningful.

5. Loyal and Dedicated

- ° Taurus is fiercely loyal and dedicated to their partner, valuing stability and consistency in their relationships.
- ° This dedication extends to their sexual life, where they are committed to pleasing their partner and maintaining a strong bond.

Common Sexual Kinks of Taurus

Taurus' sensual and submissive nature lends itself to various sexual kinks and preferences. Here are some common kinks associated with this earthy sign:

1. Sensory Play

- ° Taurus enjoys engaging all their senses during sex, making sensory play a favorite kink.
- ° Activities like blindfolding, using feathers, or incorporating scented oils can heighten their pleasure.

2. Massage and Touch

- ° This sign loves to be pampered and touched, making erotic massages a highly appealing practice.
- ° Slow, deliberate touch helps Taurus relax and fully immerse themselves in the experience.

3. Bondage

- ° Taurus often finds pleasure in being restrained, allowing them to fully submit to their partner's desires.

   ◦ Soft ropes, silk scarves, or comfortable restraints can enhance their sense of security and trust.

4. Food Play

   ◦ Given their appreciation for taste and indulgence, Taurus may enjoy incorporating food into their sexual encounters.

   ◦ Activities like feeding each other, using flavored lubricants, or engaging in playful food fights can be highly erotic.

5. Role-Playing

   ◦ Taurus enjoys stepping into different roles and scenarios, especially those that emphasize care and affection.

   ◦ Scenarios involving nurturing roles, such as a caregiver or a devoted partner, can be particularly appealing.

Recommended Kinks and Practices for Taurus

To fully satisfy a Taurus lover, it's important to cater to their sensual and submissive nature. Here are some recommended kinks and practices that can enhance their sexual experiences:

1. Erotic Massage

   ◦ Start with a slow, sensual massage to help Taurus relax and build anticipation.

   ◦ Use scented oils, soft music, and gentle touch to engage their senses and set the mood.

2. Sensory Deprivation

   ◦ Incorporate blindfolds or earplugs to heighten Taurus' remaining senses and increase their sensitivity to touch.

   ◦ This can make even the slightest touch feel more intense and pleasurable.

3. Soft Bondage

   ◦ Use soft, comfortable restraints to gently bind Taurus' wrists or ankles, allowing them to surrender control.

   ◦ Ensure that the experience is safe and consensual, creating a sense of trust and security.

4. **Food Play**
   - ° Introduce food into your sexual encounters, such as feeding each other fruits, chocolate, or whipped cream.
   - ° Use flavored body oils or edible lubricants to enhance the experience and stimulate Taurus' sense of taste.

5. **Romantic Setting**
   - ° Create a romantic atmosphere with candles, soft lighting, and soothing music.
   - ° Taurus appreciates a beautiful and comfortable environment, which can enhance their overall experience.

6. **Slow and Steady**
   - ° Take your time with Taurus, allowing for long, unhurried sessions of foreplay and lovemaking.
   - ° Focus on building a deep emotional connection through affectionate touch and loving gestures.

How Taurus is Influenced by Moon Phases, Cosmic Events, and Planetary Alignments

The sexual energy of Taurus can be further enhanced or influenced by the phases of the moon, cosmic events, and planetary alignments. Understanding these influences can help you align your sexual experiences with the cosmic rhythms.

Moon Phases

1. **New Moon**
   - ° The New Moon is a time for new beginnings and setting intentions.
   - ° Taurus can use this phase to explore new aspects of their sensuality and try out new kinks or practices.

2. **Waxing Crescent**
   - ° As the moon begins to grow, Taurus' desire for connection and intimacy increases.

- This phase is ideal for deepening emotional bonds and engaging in romantic, sensory-rich experiences.

3. **First Quarter**
   - The First Quarter Moon brings a surge of energy and determination.
   - Taurus can use this energy to take initiative in exploring their sexual desires and communicating their needs to their partner.

4. **Waxing Gibbous**
   - With the Full Moon approaching, Taurus' sensual energy builds.
   - This phase is perfect for indulging in luxurious, pampering experiences that engage all the senses.

5. **Full Moon**
   - The Full Moon heightens emotions and sexual desires, making Taurus even more passionate and affectionate.
   - This phase is ideal for deep, intimate connections and exploring fantasies that require trust and vulnerability.

6. **Waning Gibbous**
   - As the moon begins to wane, Taurus can focus on nurturing their relationship and maintaining their sexual connection.
   - Use this time for gentle, loving experiences that reinforce the bond with their partner.

7. **Last Quarter**
   - The Last Quarter Moon is a time for reassessment and letting go.
   - Taurus can release any sexual practices or dynamics that no longer serve them and explore new possibilities.

8. **Waning Crescent**
   - This final phase before the New Moon is ideal for rest and rejuvenation.

- Taurus can take this time to recharge their sexual energy and prepare for new adventures.

Cosmic Events

1. Solar Eclipses
- Solar Eclipses bring powerful shifts and transformations.
- Taurus can harness this energy to initiate significant changes in their sexual relationships and explore new dynamics.

2. Lunar Eclipses
- Lunar Eclipses heighten emotions and reveal hidden desires.
- Taurus can use this time to delve into their deepest fantasies and bring them to the surface.

3. Retrogrades
- When planets go retrograde, it's a time for reflection and reevaluation.
- Taurus can revisit past sexual experiences, learn from them, and make necessary adjustments.

4. Transits
- Transits, when planets move through different signs, bring varying influences.
- Taurus can align their sexual practices with these energies to enhance their experiences.

Planetary Alignments

1. Venus Transits
- As the ruling planet of Taurus, Venus transits significantly impact their sexual energy and romantic inclinations.
- Positive Venus transits bring harmony, beauty, and passion to their relationships.

2. **Mars Transits**
   - Mars influences desire and action, and its transits can enhance Taurus' sexual drive.
   - Positive Mars transits bring a surge of energy and enthusiasm for sexual exploration.

3. **Jupiter Transits**
   - Jupiter brings expansion and growth, which can translate to sexual exploration and indulgence.
   - Taurus may feel a desire to broaden their sexual horizons and try new things.

4. **Saturn Transits**
   - Saturn's influence can bring structure and stability to Taurus' sexual life.
   - This is a good time for setting boundaries and establishing healthy sexual practices.

By understanding the sexual characteristics, recommended practices, and cosmic influences of Taurus, you can enhance your sexual experiences and deepen your intimate connections. Embrace the sensual and submissive energy of Taurus and let it guide you to new heights of pleasure and satisfaction.

Chapter 4: Gemini - Versatile and Experimental

Sexual Characteristics and Kinks of Gemini

Gemini, the third sign of the zodiac, is ruled by Mercury, the planet of communication, intellect, and curiosity. As an air sign, Gemini is characterized by versatility, adaptability, and a constant desire for new experiences. In the realm of sexuality, Gemini is experimental, playful, and ever-changing, making their sexual encounters exciting and dynamic.

Key Sexual Characteristics of Gemini

1. **Curiosity and Experimentation**
   - Gemini's natural curiosity drives them to explore and experiment in their sexual lives.
   - They are open to trying new things and constantly seek novel experiences.

2. **Versatility**
   - Gemini is known for their adaptability and flexibility, making them versatile lovers.
   - They can easily switch between different roles and dynamics, catering to their partner's desires and their own.

3. **Playfulness**
   - This sign has a playful and light-hearted approach to sex.
   - They enjoy teasing, flirting, and incorporating fun elements into their sexual encounters.

4. **Intellectual Stimulation**
   - Gemini values mental stimulation as much as physical pleasure.
   - Engaging in witty banter, dirty talk, and role-playing scenarios can heighten their arousal.

5. **Restlessness**
   - Gemini can get bored easily and craves variety in their sexual experiences.

- ° They thrive on change and excitement, constantly seeking new adventures in the bedroom.

Common Sexual Kinks of Gemini

Gemini's versatile and experimental nature lends itself to various sexual kinks and preferences. Here are some common kinks associated with this adaptable sign:

1. **Role-Playing**
   - ° Gemini loves to step into different characters and scenarios, making role-playing a favorite kink.
   - ° They enjoy exploring different dynamics and fantasies through imaginative play.
2. **Dirty Talk**
   - ° This sign is highly verbal and finds pleasure in engaging in dirty talk.
   - ° Expressing their desires and fantasies through words can be a major turn-on for Gemini.
3. **Light Bondage**
   - ° Gemini's experimental nature makes them open to light bondage practices.
   - ° Using cuffs, blindfolds, or silk scarves can add excitement and variety to their experiences.
4. **Voyeurism and Exhibitionism**
   - ° Gemini enjoys the thrill of being watched and watching others.
   - ° Incorporating elements of voyeurism or exhibitionism can enhance their arousal.
5. **Sensory Play**
   - ° This sign is intrigued by sensory experiences and enjoys exploring different sensations.
   - ° Using feathers, ice, or silk can heighten their pleasure and add variety to their encounters.

Recommended Kinks and Practices for Gemini

To fully satisfy a Gemini lover, it's important to cater to their versatile and experimental nature. Here are some recommended kinks and practices that can enhance their sexual experiences:

1. **Role-Playing Scenarios**
   - Create various role-playing scenarios that allow Gemini to explore different characters and fantasies.
   - Encourage their creativity and imagination by introducing new roles and storylines regularly.

2. **Dirty Talk**
   - Engage in dirty talk to stimulate Gemini's mind and enhance their arousal.
   - Share fantasies, describe actions, and use playful banter to keep things exciting.

3. **Light Bondage**
   - Introduce light bondage elements such as handcuffs, blindfolds, or silk ties.
   - Ensure that the experience is safe, consensual, and adds a sense of adventure and excitement.

4. **Voyeuristic Activities**
   - Incorporate voyeuristic or exhibitionistic elements into your encounters.
   - Watching erotic films together, attending adult parties, or simply being intimate in semi-public places can be thrilling for Gemini.

5. **Sensory Exploration**
   - Use various sensory tools to create a range of tactile experiences.
   - Feathers, ice cubes, massage oils, and textured fabrics can add an element of surprise and novelty.

6. Change and Variety

- Keep things fresh and exciting by regularly introducing new activities, positions, and locations.
- Gemini thrives on variety, so avoid falling into routine and always be open to new experiences.

How Gemini is Influenced by Moon Phases, Cosmic Events, and Planetary Alignments

The sexual energy of Gemini can be further enhanced or influenced by the phases of the moon, cosmic events, and planetary alignments. Understanding these influences can help you align your sexual experiences with the cosmic rhythms.

Moon Phases

1. New Moon

- The New Moon is a time for new beginnings and setting intentions.
- Gemini can use this phase to explore new sexual practices or initiate a fresh dynamic in their relationship.

2. Waxing Crescent

- As the moon begins to grow, so does Gemini's desire for experimentation and novelty.
- This phase is ideal for planning new sexual adventures and trying out different kinks.

3. First Quarter

- The First Quarter Moon brings a surge of energy and determination.
- Gemini can harness this energy to take initiative in exploring their sexual desires and communicating their needs to their partner.

4. Waxing Gibbous

- With the Full Moon approaching, Gemini's sexual energy and excitement build.

- This is a great time for engaging in intense and playful encounters that involve a lot of variety.

5. Full Moon

- The Full Moon heightens emotions and sexual desires, making Gemini even more adventurous and experimental.
- This phase is perfect for indulging in bold and daring sexual activities.

6. Waning Gibbous

- As the moon begins to wane, Gemini can focus on reflecting and deepening their sexual connection.
- Use this time for intimate and meaningful experiences that reinforce the bond with their partner.

7. Last Quarter

- The Last Quarter Moon is a time for reassessment and letting go.
- Gemini can release any sexual practices or dynamics that no longer serve them and explore new possibilities.

8. Waning Crescent

- This final phase before the New Moon is ideal for rest and rejuvenation.
- Gemini can take this time to recharge their sexual energy and prepare for new adventures.

Cosmic Events

1. Solar Eclipses

- Solar Eclipses bring powerful shifts and transformations.
- Gemini can harness this energy to initiate significant changes in their sexual relationships and explore new dynamics.

2. Lunar Eclipses

- Lunar Eclipses heighten emotions and reveal hidden desires.

- Gemini can use this time to delve into their deepest fantasies and bring them to the surface.

3. **Retrogrades**
   - When planets go retrograde, it's a time for reflection and reevaluation.
   - Gemini can revisit past sexual experiences, learn from them, and make necessary adjustments.

4. **Transits**
   - Transits, when planets move through different signs, bring varying influences.
   - Gemini can align their sexual practices with these energies to enhance their experiences.

Planetary Alignments

1. **Mercury Transits**
   - As the ruling planet of Gemini, Mercury transits significantly impact their sexual energy and communication.
   - Positive Mercury transits bring clarity, wit, and a heightened ability to express desires and fantasies.

2. **Venus Transits**
   - Venus influences love and pleasure, and its transits can enhance Gemini's romantic and sexual experiences.
   - Positive Venus transits bring harmony and excitement to their relationships.

3. **Mars Transits**
   - Mars influences desire and action, and its transits can enhance Gemini's sexual drive.
   - Positive Mars transits bring a surge of energy and enthusiasm for sexual exploration.

4. **Jupiter Transits**
   - Jupiter brings expansion and growth, which can translate to sexual exploration and indulgence.

- Gemini may feel a desire to broaden their sexual horizons and try new things.

By understanding the sexual characteristics, recommended practices, and cosmic influences of Gemini, you can enhance your sexual experiences and deepen your intimate connections. Embrace the versatile and experimental energy of Gemini and let it guide you to new heights of pleasure and excitement.

Chapter 5: Cancer - Nurturing and Emotional

Sexual Characteristics and Kinks of Cancer

Cancer, the fourth sign of the zodiac, is ruled by the moon, which governs emotions, instincts, and subconscious desires. As a water sign, Cancer is deeply intuitive, sensitive, and emotionally driven. In the realm of sexuality, Cancer is nurturing, affectionate, and seeks profound emotional connections. Their sexual encounters are often intimate, tender, and rooted in love and care.

Key Sexual Characteristics of Cancer

1. **Emotional Depth**
   - Cancer experiences sex as an emotional and spiritual connection, valuing intimacy and closeness.
   - They are highly attuned to their partner's needs and emotions, creating a safe and comforting environment.

2. **Nurturing Nature**
   - Cancer is naturally nurturing and enjoys taking care of their partner's needs, both in and out of the bedroom.
   - They find pleasure in providing comfort, affection, and emotional support during sexual encounters.

3. **Affectionate and Tender**
   - This sign is known for its gentle and loving approach to sex.
   - Cancer values cuddling, kissing, and other forms of affectionate touch that enhance their emotional bond.

4. **Intuitive and Sensitive**
   - Cancer has a strong intuitive sense, allowing them to understand their partner's desires and emotions without needing words.
   - They are sensitive to touch and can be easily aroused by emotional and physical closeness.

5. Protective and Loyal
- ○ Cancer is fiercely loyal and protective of their partner, creating a sense of security and trust.
- ○ They are dedicated lovers who prioritize their partner's well-being and happiness.

Common Sexual Kinks of Cancer

Cancer's nurturing and emotional nature lends itself to various sexual kinks and preferences. Here are some common kinks associated with this sensitive sign:

1. Sensual Play
- ○ Cancer enjoys slow, sensual experiences that involve affectionate touch and emotional connection.
- ○ Activities like massage, kissing, and gentle caresses are highly pleasurable for them.

2. Role-Playing
- ○ This sign may enjoy role-playing scenarios that emphasize nurturing and caregiving roles.
- ○ Scenarios such as nurse/patient or teacher/student can be particularly appealing.

3. Emotional Bondage
- ○ Cancer may find pleasure in forms of bondage that emphasize trust and emotional surrender.
- ○ Using soft restraints or being held closely can enhance their sense of security and intimacy.

4. Cuddling and Aftercare
- ○ Aftercare is essential for Cancer, as they value the emotional connection that comes from cuddling and comforting their partner after sex.

- Engaging in prolonged cuddling sessions and providing emotional support is deeply satisfying for them.

5. **Home-Based Fantasies**
   - Cancer often feels most comfortable and aroused in the familiarity of their home environment.
   - Fantasies and role-plays that take place in domestic settings, such as the kitchen or bedroom, can be particularly stimulating.

Recommended Kinks and Practices for Cancer

To fully satisfy a Cancer lover, it's important to cater to their nurturing and emotional nature. Here are some recommended kinks and practices that can enhance their sexual experiences:

1. **Sensual Massage**
   - Begin with a slow, sensual massage to help Cancer relax and feel cared for.
   - Use scented oils, soft music, and gentle touch to create a calming and intimate atmosphere.

2. **Emotional Connection**
   - Prioritize emotional connection and communication during sex.
   - Share feelings, express love and affection, and ensure that Cancer feels emotionally secure and valued.

3. **Affectionate Touch**
   - Incorporate plenty of affectionate touch, such as kissing, cuddling, and gentle caresses.
   - Focus on creating a tender and loving experience that enhances emotional intimacy.

4. **Role-Playing Scenarios**
   - Introduce role-playing scenarios that involve nurturing and caregiving dynamics.

- ° Encourage Cancer's creativity and empathy by exploring different roles and fantasies.

5. **Comfort and Security**
   - ° Ensure that Cancer feels comfortable and secure in their environment.
   - ° Create a cozy and familiar setting, using soft blankets, pillows, and soothing lighting.

6. **Aftercare and Cuddling**
   - ° Emphasize the importance of aftercare and cuddling after sex.
   - ° Spend time holding and comforting each other, reinforcing the emotional connection and providing reassurance.

How Cancer is Influenced by Moon Phases, Cosmic Events, and Planetary Alignments

The sexual energy of Cancer can be further enhanced or influenced by the phases of the moon, cosmic events, and planetary alignments. Understanding these influences can help you align your sexual experiences with the cosmic rhythms.

Moon Phases

1. **New Moon**
   - ° The New Moon is a time for new beginnings and setting intentions.
   - ° Cancer can use this phase to explore new aspects of their sexuality and deepen their emotional bond with their partner.

2. **Waxing Crescent**
   - ° As the moon begins to grow, Cancer's desire for intimacy and connection increases.

- This phase is ideal for nurturing emotional and physical closeness in their sexual experiences.

3. **First Quarter**
   - The First Quarter Moon brings a surge of energy and determination.
   - Cancer can use this energy to take initiative in expressing their desires and enhancing their sexual relationships.

4. **Waxing Gibbous**
   - With the Full Moon approaching, Cancer's emotional and sexual energy builds.
   - This is a great time for engaging in deeply intimate and affectionate encounters.

5. **Full Moon**
   - The Full Moon heightens emotions and sexual desires, making Cancer even more nurturing and loving.
   - This phase is perfect for indulging in tender, romantic, and emotionally fulfilling sexual activities.

6. **Waning Gibbous**
   - As the moon begins to wane, Cancer can focus on maintaining and nurturing their emotional connection.
   - Use this time for gentle, loving experiences that reinforce the bond with their partner.

7. **Last Quarter**
   - The Last Quarter Moon is a time for reassessment and letting go.
   - Cancer can release any sexual practices or dynamics that no longer serve them and explore new possibilities.

8. **Waning Crescent**
   - This final phase before the New Moon is ideal for rest and rejuvenation.
   - Cancer can take this time to recharge their emotional and sexual energy and prepare for new adventures.

Cosmic Events

1. **Solar Eclipses**
   - Solar Eclipses bring powerful shifts and transformations.
   - Cancer can harness this energy to initiate significant changes in their sexual relationships and explore new dynamics.
2. **Lunar Eclipses**
   - Lunar Eclipses heighten emotions and reveal hidden desires.
   - Cancer can use this time to delve into their deepest fantasies and bring them to the surface.
3. **Retrogrades**
   - When planets go retrograde, it's a time for reflection and reevaluation.
   - Cancer can revisit past sexual experiences, learn from them, and make necessary adjustments.
4. **Transits**
   - Transits, when planets move through different signs, bring varying influences.
   - Cancer can align their sexual practices with these energies to enhance their experiences.

Planetary Alignments

1. **Moon Transits**
   - As the ruling celestial body of Cancer, the moon's transits significantly impact their emotional and sexual energy.
   - Positive moon transits bring heightened sensitivity, intuition, and a strong desire for intimacy.
2. **Venus Transits**
   - Venus influences love and pleasure, and its transits can enhance Cancer's romantic and sexual experiences.

- ° Positive Venus transits bring harmony, beauty, and emotional fulfillment to their relationships.

3. **Mars Transits**
   - ° Mars influences desire and action, and its transits can enhance Cancer's sexual drive.
   - ° Positive Mars transits bring a surge of energy and enthusiasm for sexual exploration.

4. **Jupiter Transits**
   - ° Jupiter brings expansion and growth, which can translate to sexual exploration and indulgence.
   - ° Cancer may feel a desire to broaden their sexual horizons and try new things.

By understanding the sexual characteristics, recommended practices, and cosmic influences of Cancer, you can enhance your sexual experiences and deepen your intimate connections. Embrace the nurturing and emotional energy of Cancer and let it guide you to new heights of pleasure and emotional fulfillment.

Chapter 6: Leo - Confident and Theatrical
Sexual Characteristics and Kinks of Leo

Leo, the fifth sign of the zodiac, is ruled by the sun, which symbolizes vitality, confidence, and self-expression. As a fire sign, Leo is passionate, bold, and loves to be the center of attention. In the realm of sexuality, Leo is confident, playful, and enjoys making a dramatic impression. Their sexual encounters are often intense, passionate, and filled with a sense of grandeur and theatrics.

Key Sexual Characteristics of Leo

1. **Confidence and Charisma**
   - Leo exudes confidence and charisma, making them irresistible to their partners.
   - They are self-assured lovers who take pride in their sexual prowess and abilities.
2. **Theatrical and Dramatic**
   - Leo enjoys bringing a sense of drama and excitement to their sexual encounters.
   - They often see sex as a performance and love to captivate and entertain their partner.
3. **Passionate and Intense**
   - This sign is known for its intense passion and high libido.
   - Leo loves to express their desires fully and expects the same level of enthusiasm from their partner.
4. **Playful and Fun-Loving**
   - Leo has a playful and adventurous approach to sex.
   - They enjoy incorporating fun elements, such as costumes, role-playing, and games, into their sexual experiences.
5. **Attention-Seeking**
   - Leo loves to be admired and adored, both in and out of the bedroom.

◦ They thrive on compliments and praise, and they want to feel like the star of the show during sex.

Common Sexual Kinks of Leo

Leo's confident and theatrical nature lends itself to various sexual kinks and preferences. Here are some common kinks associated with this bold sign:

1. **Role-Playing**
    ◦ Leo loves to step into different characters and scenarios, making role-playing a favorite kink.
    ◦ They enjoy exploring different dynamics and fantasies through imaginative play.
2. **Exhibitionism**
    ◦ This sign enjoys being watched and showing off their sexual prowess.
    ◦ Engaging in sexual activities in front of a mirror or in semi-public places can be highly arousing for Leo.
3. **Power Play**
    ◦ Leo often enjoys taking on dominant roles in power play dynamics.
    ◦ They find pleasure in exerting control and guiding their partner through intense experiences.
4. **Costumes and Props**
    ◦ Incorporating costumes, props, and theatrical elements into their sexual encounters can be highly stimulating for Leo.
    ◦ They enjoy adding a sense of drama and excitement to their experiences.
5. **Praise and Worship**
    ◦ Leo thrives on compliments and adoration from their partner.

- ° They enjoy being praised and worshipped for their sexual skills and attractiveness.

Recommended Kinks and Practices for Leo

To fully satisfy a Leo lover, it's important to cater to their confident and theatrical nature. Here are some recommended kinks and practices that can enhance their sexual experiences:

1. **Role-Playing Scenarios**
    - ° Create various role-playing scenarios that allow Leo to explore different characters and fantasies.
    - ° Encourage their creativity and theatrical flair by introducing new roles and storylines regularly.

2. **Exhibitionistic Activities**
    - ° Incorporate elements of exhibitionism into your encounters, such as having sex in front of a mirror or engaging in semi-public activities.
    - ° Make Leo feel admired and desired by appreciating their performance and confidence.

3. **Power Play Dynamics**
    - ° Engage in power play dynamics where Leo can take on a dominant role.
    - ° Use commands, restraints, and other elements of control to enhance their sense of power and confidence.

4. **Costumes and Props**
    - ° Introduce costumes, props, and theatrical elements into your sexual experiences.
    - ° Encourage Leo to express their dramatic side through fun and imaginative scenarios.

5. **Praise and Worship**
    - ° Shower Leo with compliments and praise during and after sex.

- Make them feel like the star of the show by appreciating their skills, attractiveness, and confidence.

6. **Playful and Adventurous Activities**
    - Keep things exciting and fun by incorporating games, challenges, and adventurous activities into your sexual encounters.
    - Leo thrives on excitement and variety, so avoid falling into routine and always be open to new experiences.

How Leo is Influenced by Moon Phases, Cosmic Events, and Planetary Alignments

The sexual energy of Leo can be further enhanced or influenced by the phases of the moon, cosmic events, and planetary alignments. Understanding these influences can help you align your sexual experiences with the cosmic rhythms.

Moon Phases

1. **New Moon**
    - The New Moon is a time for new beginnings and setting intentions.
    - Leo can use this phase to explore new aspects of their sexuality and initiate fresh dynamics in their relationship.

2. **Waxing Crescent**
    - As the moon begins to grow, so does Leo's desire for excitement and experimentation.
    - This phase is ideal for planning new sexual adventures and trying out different kinks.

3. **First Quarter**
    - The First Quarter Moon brings a surge of energy and determination.

- Leo can harness this energy to take initiative in expressing their desires and enhancing their sexual relationships.

4. **Waxing Gibbous**
   - With the Full Moon approaching, Leo's sexual energy and excitement build.
   - This is a great time for engaging in intense and dramatic encounters that involve a lot of creativity and flair.

5. **Full Moon**
   - The Full Moon heightens emotions and sexual desires, making Leo even more passionate and theatrical.
   - This phase is perfect for indulging in bold and daring sexual activities that showcase their confidence and performance skills.

6. **Waning Gibbous**
   - As the moon begins to wane, Leo can focus on maintaining and nurturing their sexual connection.
   - Use this time for playful and loving experiences that reinforce the bond with their partner.

7. **Last Quarter**
   - The Last Quarter Moon is a time for reassessment and letting go.
   - Leo can release any sexual practices or dynamics that no longer serve them and explore new possibilities.

8. **Waning Crescent**
   - This final phase before the New Moon is ideal for rest and rejuvenation.
   - Leo can take this time to recharge their sexual energy and prepare for new adventures.

Cosmic Events

1. **Solar Eclipses**
   - Solar Eclipses bring powerful shifts and transformations.

- Leo can harness this energy to initiate significant changes in their sexual relationships and explore new dynamics.

2. **Lunar Eclipses**
   - Lunar Eclipses heighten emotions and reveal hidden desires.
   - Leo can use this time to delve into their deepest fantasies and bring them to the surface.

3. **Retrogrades**
   - When planets go retrograde, it's a time for reflection and reevaluation.
   - Leo can revisit past sexual experiences, learn from them, and make necessary adjustments.

4. **Transits**
   - Transits, when planets move through different signs, bring varying influences.
   - Leo can align their sexual practices with these energies to enhance their experiences.

Planetary Alignments

1. **Sun Transits**
   - As the ruling celestial body of Leo, the sun's transits significantly impact their vitality and sexual energy.
   - Positive sun transits bring heightened confidence, charisma, and a strong desire for self-expression.

2. **Venus Transits**
   - Venus influences love and pleasure, and its transits can enhance Leo's romantic and sexual experiences.
   - Positive Venus transits bring harmony, beauty, and a heightened sense of romance and passion.

3. **Mars Transits**
   - Mars influences desire and action, and its transits can enhance Leo's sexual drive.

- ○ Positive Mars transits bring a surge of energy, enthusiasm, and a desire for bold and adventurous sexual exploration.
4. **Jupiter Transits**
   - ○ Jupiter brings expansion and growth, which can translate to sexual exploration and indulgence.
   - ○ Leo may feel a desire to broaden their sexual horizons and try new things.

By understanding the sexual characteristics, recommended practices, and cosmic influences of Leo, you can enhance your sexual experiences and deepen your intimate connections. Embrace the confident and theatrical energy of Leo and let it guide you to new heights of pleasure and excitement.

Chapter 7: Virgo - Precise and Discreet
Sexual Characteristics and Kinks of Virgo

Virgo, the sixth sign of the zodiac, is ruled by Mercury, the planet of communication, intellect, and detail. As an earth sign, Virgo is practical, meticulous, and grounded. In the realm of sexuality, Virgo is precise, discreet, and attentive to detail, often approaching intimacy with a blend of careful consideration and a desire for perfection. Their sexual encounters are characterized by a focus on pleasing their partner and ensuring a high-quality experience.

Key Sexual Characteristics of Virgo

1. **Attention to Detail**
   - Virgo pays close attention to the nuances of their partner's desires and needs.
   - They strive for perfection in their sexual performance and aim to create a flawless experience.
2. **Discreet and Private**
   - Virgo values privacy and discretion in their sexual encounters.
   - They are not typically exhibitionists and prefer intimate, private settings for their activities.
3. **Intellectual Stimulation**
   - This sign finds intellectual connection and communication highly arousing.
   - Engaging in meaningful conversation and mental foreplay can significantly enhance their sexual experience.
4. **Service-Oriented**
   - Virgo derives pleasure from being of service and pleasing their partner.

- They are attentive lovers who prioritize their partner's satisfaction and well-being.

5. **Practical and Methodical**
   - Virgo approaches sex in a practical and methodical manner, often planning and considering every detail.
   - They appreciate routines and practices that ensure a clean and comfortable environment.

Common Sexual Kinks of Virgo

Virgo's precise and discreet nature lends itself to various sexual kinks and preferences. Here are some common kinks associated with this meticulous sign:

1. **Sensory Play**
   - Virgo enjoys sensory experiences that involve subtle and refined touch.
   - Activities like light spanking, gentle caresses, and sensory deprivation can heighten their pleasure.

2. **Role-Playing**
   - This sign may enjoy role-playing scenarios that involve service and submission dynamics.
   - Scenarios such as maid/butler or teacher/student can be particularly appealing.

3. **Clean and Hygienic Practices**
   - Virgo has a strong preference for cleanliness and hygiene.
   - Incorporating activities that emphasize cleanliness, such as erotic baths or showers, can be highly satisfying.

4. **Erotic Massage**
   - Virgo appreciates the detailed and intimate nature of erotic massages.

- ◦ Using scented oils and focusing on different parts of the body can create a deeply relaxing and arousing experience.

5. **Mutual Masturbation**
    - ◦ Virgo finds pleasure in mutual masturbation, where both partners can explore their bodies in a controlled and private manner.
    - ◦ This allows them to maintain a sense of control while experiencing intimacy.

Recommended Kinks and Practices for Virgo

To fully satisfy a Virgo lover, it's important to cater to their precise and discreet nature. Here are some recommended kinks and practices that can enhance their sexual experiences:

1. **Sensory Play**
    - ◦ Engage in sensory play that involves light and refined touch.
    - ◦ Use feathers, silk, or soft brushes to stimulate their senses and create a subtle but intense experience.
2. **Erotic Massage**
    - ◦ Begin with a slow, methodical erotic massage to help Virgo relax and feel cared for.
    - ◦ Use scented oils and focus on different parts of their body, paying attention to their responses.
3. **Role-Playing Scenarios**
    - ◦ Introduce role-playing scenarios that involve service-oriented dynamics.
    - ◦ Encourage Virgo to step into roles that align with their meticulous and attentive nature.
4. **Clean and Hygienic Practices**
    - ◦ Emphasize cleanliness and hygiene in your sexual encounters.

- ° Incorporate activities like shared showers or baths, ensuring a fresh and comfortable environment.

5. **Intellectual Stimulation**
   - ° Engage in meaningful conversation and mental foreplay to stimulate Virgo's mind.
   - ° Share fantasies, discuss desires, and use articulate language to enhance their arousal.

6. **Mutual Masturbation**
   - ° Practice mutual masturbation to allow Virgo to explore their body in a controlled and private manner.
   - ° Encourage open communication about what feels good and use this as an opportunity to learn more about each other.

How Virgo is Influenced by Moon Phases, Cosmic Events, and Planetary Alignments

The sexual energy of Virgo can be further enhanced or influenced by the phases of the moon, cosmic events, and planetary alignments. Understanding these influences can help you align your sexual experiences with the cosmic rhythms.

Moon Phases

1. **New Moon**
   - ° The New Moon is a time for new beginnings and setting intentions.
   - ° Virgo can use this phase to explore new aspects of their sexuality and initiate fresh dynamics in their relationship.

2. **Waxing Crescent**
   - ° As the moon begins to grow, so does Virgo's desire for connection and intimacy.

- ◦ This phase is ideal for planning new sexual adventures and trying out different kinks.

3. **First Quarter**

- ◦ The First Quarter Moon brings a surge of energy and determination.
- ◦ Virgo can harness this energy to take initiative in expressing their desires and enhancing their sexual relationships.

4. **Waxing Gibbous**

- ◦ With the Full Moon approaching, Virgo's sexual energy and excitement build.
- ◦ This is a great time for engaging in intense and detailed encounters that involve a lot of precision and care.

5. **Full Moon**

- ◦ The Full Moon heightens emotions and sexual desires, making Virgo even more attentive and dedicated to their partner.
- ◦ This phase is perfect for indulging in detailed and methodical sexual activities that showcase their precision and care.

6. **Waning Gibbous**

- ◦ As the moon begins to wane, Virgo can focus on maintaining and nurturing their sexual connection.
- ◦ Use this time for gentle and loving experiences that reinforce the bond with their partner.

7. **Last Quarter**

- ◦ The Last Quarter Moon is a time for reassessment and letting go.
- ◦ Virgo can release any sexual practices or dynamics that no longer serve them and explore new possibilities.

8. **Waning Crescent**

- ◦ This final phase before the New Moon is ideal for rest and rejuvenation.
- ◦ Virgo can take this time to recharge their sexual energy and prepare for new adventures.

Cosmic Events

1. Solar Eclipses
- Solar Eclipses bring powerful shifts and transformations.
- Virgo can harness this energy to initiate significant changes in their sexual relationships and explore new dynamics.

2. Lunar Eclipses
- Lunar Eclipses heighten emotions and reveal hidden desires.
- Virgo can use this time to delve into their deepest fantasies and bring them to the surface.

3. Retrogrades
- When planets go retrograde, it's a time for reflection and reevaluation.
- Virgo can revisit past sexual experiences, learn from them, and make necessary adjustments.

4. Transits
- Transits, when planets move through different signs, bring varying influences.
- Virgo can align their sexual practices with these energies to enhance their experiences.

Planetary Alignments

1. Mercury Transits
- As the ruling planet of Virgo, Mercury transits significantly impact their intellectual and sexual energy.
- Positive Mercury transits bring clarity, attention to detail, and a heightened ability to communicate desires and fantasies.

2. Venus Transits
- Venus influences love and pleasure, and its transits can enhance Virgo's romantic and sexual experiences.

- ° Positive Venus transits bring harmony, beauty, and a heightened sense of romance and intimacy.

3. **Mars Transits**
    - ° Mars influences desire and action, and its transits can enhance Virgo's sexual drive.
    - ° Positive Mars transits bring a surge of energy, enthusiasm, and a desire for precise and methodical sexual exploration.

4. **Saturn Transits**
    - ° Saturn's influence can bring structure and discipline to Virgo's sexual life.
    - ° This is a good time for setting boundaries and establishing healthy sexual practices.

By understanding the sexual characteristics, recommended practices, and cosmic influences of Virgo, you can enhance your sexual experiences and deepen your intimate connections. Embrace the precise and discreet energy of Virgo and let it guide you to new heights of pleasure and satisfaction.

Chapter 8: Libra - Balanced and Romantic
Sexual Characteristics and Kinks of Libra

Libra, the seventh sign of the zodiac, is ruled by Venus, the planet of love, beauty, and harmony. As an air sign, Libra is sociable, charming, and seeks balance and fairness in all aspects of life, including their sexuality. In the realm of sexuality, Libra is romantic, attentive, and values mutual satisfaction. Their sexual encounters are characterized by a desire for balance, elegance, and a deep connection with their partner.

Key Sexual Characteristics of Libra

1. **Romantic and Charming**
   - Libra approaches sex with a romantic and charming demeanor.
   - They enjoy creating a beautiful and harmonious atmosphere, often incorporating elements of romance and elegance into their encounters.

2. **Balanced and Fair**
   - This sign values balance and fairness, striving for mutual satisfaction in their sexual relationships.
   - Libra is attentive to their partner's needs and desires, ensuring that both parties experience pleasure.

3. **Aesthetic and Sensual**
   - Libra has a heightened appreciation for aesthetics and beauty, which extends to their sexual experiences.
   - They enjoy visually pleasing settings, lingerie, and sensual activities that engage multiple senses.

4. **Sociable and Communicative**
   - Libra is naturally sociable and enjoys open communication with their partner.
   - They find intellectual and verbal stimulation arousing, often engaging in flirtatious banter and seductive conversations.

5. **Diplomatic and Considerate**
   - Libra is diplomatic and considerate, always aiming to create a positive and harmonious experience.
   - They avoid conflict and prefer to resolve any issues with grace and tact.

Common Sexual Kinks of Libra

Libra's balanced and romantic nature lends itself to various sexual kinks and preferences. Here are some common kinks associated with this charming sign:

1. **Role-Playing**
   - Libra enjoys role-playing scenarios that emphasize romance, elegance, and balance.
   - Scenarios such as prince/princess, artist/muse, or other romantic fantasies can be particularly appealing.
2. **Sensory Play**
   - This sign is highly sensual and enjoys engaging in sensory play.
   - Activities like using scented candles, silk fabrics, or sensual oils can enhance their pleasure.
3. **Erotic Massage**
   - Libra appreciates the intimate and soothing nature of erotic massages.
   - Incorporating gentle touch and sensual oils can create a deeply relaxing and arousing experience.
4. **Romantic Settings**
   - Creating romantic settings with candles, soft music, and beautiful decor can be highly stimulating for Libra.
   - They enjoy environments that reflect harmony and beauty, enhancing their sexual experience.

5. Power Play (Balanced)

- While Libra values balance, they can enjoy light power play that involves a fair and equal exchange of roles.
- Activities like taking turns being in control can add excitement while maintaining harmony.

Recommended Kinks and Practices for Libra

To fully satisfy a Libra lover, it's important to cater to their balanced and romantic nature. Here are some recommended kinks and practices that can enhance their sexual experiences:

1. Role-Playing Scenarios

- Create various role-playing scenarios that emphasize romance and elegance.
- Encourage Libra to explore different characters and fantasies that align with their charming and balanced nature.

2. Sensory Play

- Engage in sensory play that involves visually and tactilely pleasing elements.
- Use scented candles, silk fabrics, and sensual oils to create a beautiful and stimulating environment.

3. Erotic Massage

- Begin with a slow, sensual erotic massage to help Libra relax and feel cared for.
- Use scented oils and focus on creating a harmonious and intimate atmosphere.

4. Romantic Settings

- Create romantic settings with candles, soft music, and elegant decor.
- Libra will appreciate the effort put into creating a beautiful and harmonious environment.

5. **Balanced Power Play**
    ◦ Introduce light power play dynamics that involve a fair and equal exchange of roles.
    ◦ Take turns being in control and ensure that both partners feel balanced and satisfied.

6. **Open Communication**
    ◦ Engage in open and honest communication about desires and boundaries.
    ◦ Libra values intellectual and verbal stimulation, so discussing fantasies and preferences can enhance their arousal.

How Libra is Influenced by Moon Phases, Cosmic Events, and Planetary Alignments

The sexual energy of Libra can be further enhanced or influenced by the phases of the moon, cosmic events, and planetary alignments. Understanding these influences can help you align your sexual experiences with the cosmic rhythms.

Moon Phases

1. **New Moon**
    ◦ The New Moon is a time for new beginnings and setting intentions.
    ◦ Libra can use this phase to explore new aspects of their sexuality and initiate fresh dynamics in their relationship.

2. **Waxing Crescent**
    ◦ As the moon begins to grow, so does Libra's desire for connection and harmony.
    ◦ This phase is ideal for planning romantic and balanced sexual encounters.

3. **First Quarter**
    ◦ The First Quarter Moon brings a surge of energy and determination.

- Libra can harness this energy to take initiative in expressing their desires and enhancing their sexual relationships.

4. **Waxing Gibbous**
   - With the Full Moon approaching, Libra's sexual energy and excitement build.
   - This is a great time for engaging in intense and romantic encounters that involve a lot of elegance and charm.

5. **Full Moon**
   - The Full Moon heightens emotions and sexual desires, making Libra even more romantic and attentive.
   - This phase is perfect for indulging in passionate and balanced sexual activities that showcase their charm and grace.

6. **Waning Gibbous**
   - As the moon begins to wane, Libra can focus on maintaining and nurturing their sexual connection.
   - Use this time for gentle and loving experiences that reinforce the bond with their partner.

7. **Last Quarter**
   - The Last Quarter Moon is a time for reassessment and letting go.
   - Libra can release any sexual practices or dynamics that no longer serve them and explore new possibilities.

8. **Waning Crescent**
   - This final phase before the New Moon is ideal for rest and rejuvenation.
   - Libra can take this time to recharge their sexual energy and prepare for new adventures.

Cosmic Events

1. **Solar Eclipses**
   - Solar Eclipses bring powerful shifts and transformations.

- Libra can harness this energy to initiate significant changes in their sexual relationships and explore new dynamics.

2. **Lunar Eclipses**
   - Lunar Eclipses heighten emotions and reveal hidden desires.
   - Libra can use this time to delve into their deepest fantasies and bring them to the surface.

3. **Retrogrades**
   - When planets go retrograde, it's a time for reflection and reevaluation.
   - Libra can revisit past sexual experiences, learn from them, and make necessary adjustments.

4. **Transits**
   - Transits, when planets move through different signs, bring varying influences.
   - Libra can align their sexual practices with these energies to enhance their experiences.

Planetary Alignments

1. **Venus Transits**
   - As the ruling planet of Libra, Venus transits significantly impact their romantic and sexual energy.
   - Positive Venus transits bring harmony, beauty, and a heightened sense of romance and pleasure.

2. **Mercury Transits**
   - Mercury influences communication and intellect, and its transits can enhance Libra's ability to articulate desires and fantasies.
   - Positive Mercury transits bring clarity and eloquence to their sexual communication.

3. **Mars Transits**
- ° Mars influences desire and action, and its transits can enhance Libra's sexual drive.
- ° Positive Mars transits bring a surge of energy, enthusiasm, and a desire for balanced and passionate sexual exploration.

4. **Jupiter Transits**
- ° Jupiter brings expansion and growth, which can translate to sexual exploration and indulgence.
- ° Libra may feel a desire to broaden their sexual horizons and try new things.

By understanding the sexual characteristics, recommended practices, and cosmic influences of Libra, you can enhance your sexual experiences and deepen your intimate connections. Embrace the balanced and romantic energy of Libra and let it guide you to new heights of pleasure and satisfaction.

Chapter 9: Scorpio - Intense and Passionate
Sexual Characteristics and Kinks of Scorpio

Scorpio, the eighth sign of the zodiac, is ruled by both Mars, the planet of passion and aggression, and Pluto, the planet of transformation and power. As a water sign, Scorpio is deeply emotional, intuitive, and driven by a need for intensity and depth in all aspects of life, including their sexuality. In the realm of sexuality, Scorpio is passionate, intense, and often explores the darker, more mysterious aspects of sexual experiences.

Key Sexual Characteristics of Scorpio

1. **Intensity and Passion**
   - Scorpio experiences sex with intense passion and depth.
   - They are highly driven by their desires and seek to create profound and transformative sexual encounters.

2. **Emotional Depth**
   - This sign values emotional connection and intimacy in their sexual relationships.
   - Scorpio secks to understand their partner on a deep, emotional level, often creating strong and lasting bonds.

3. **Magnetic and Mysterious**
   - Scorpio has a magnetic and mysterious allure that draws others in.
   - They often exude an air of mystery and sensuality that can be highly captivating.

4. **Dominant and Controlling**
   - Scorpio often enjoys taking on a dominant role in their sexual encounters.
   - They find pleasure in control and power dynamics, seeking to guide and influence their partner's experiences.

5. **Explorative and Experimental**
   - This sign is open to exploring a wide range of sexual activities and kinks.
   - Scorpio is unafraid to delve into taboo or unconventional practices, always seeking new depths of pleasure.

Common Sexual Kinks of Scorpio

Scorpio's intense and passionate nature lends itself to various sexual kinks and preferences. Here are some common kinks associated with this powerful sign:

1. **BDSM**
   - Scorpio often enjoys BDSM practices, including bondage, dominance, submission, and sadomasochism.
   - They find pleasure in power dynamics and the intensity of these experiences.
2. **Role-Playing**
   - This sign enjoys role-playing scenarios that involve elements of control, mystery, and power.
   - Scenarios such as master/slave or secret agent/spy can be particularly appealing.
3. **Sensory Deprivation**
   - Scorpio is intrigued by sensory deprivation practices, such as blindfolding and using earplugs.
   - These activities heighten their other senses and create a deeper sense of connection and intensity.
4. **Tantric Sex**
   - Scorpio may be drawn to tantric practices that emphasize prolonged intimacy and deep emotional connection.
   - These practices align with their desire for transformative and profound sexual experiences.

5. Voyeurism and Exhibitionism

- ○ Scorpio enjoys the thrill of being watched or watching others.
- ○ Incorporating elements of voyeurism or exhibitionism can enhance their arousal and excitement.

Recommended Kinks and Practices for Scorpio

To fully satisfy a Scorpio lover, it's important to cater to their intense and passionate nature. Here are some recommended kinks and practices that can enhance their sexual experiences:

1. BDSM Dynamics

- ○ Engage in BDSM practices that involve elements of dominance, submission, and power play.
- ○ Use restraints, blindfolds, and commands to create an intense and thrilling experience.

2. Role-Playing Scenarios

- ○ Create various role-playing scenarios that involve control, mystery, and power dynamics.
- ○ Encourage Scorpio to explore different roles and fantasies that align with their passionate nature.

3. Sensory Deprivation

- ○ Incorporate sensory deprivation practices to heighten Scorpio's other senses.
- ○ Use blindfolds, earplugs, or other tools to create a deeper sense of connection and intensity.

4. Tantric Practices

- ○ Explore tantric sex practices that emphasize prolonged intimacy and deep emotional connection.
- ○ Focus on breathing techniques, eye contact, and slow, deliberate movements to create a transformative experience.

5. **Voyeurism and Exhibitionism**
    - Introduce elements of voyeurism or exhibitionism into your encounters.
    - Watching erotic films together, attending adult parties, or simply being intimate in semi-public places can be thrilling for Scorpio.

6. **Deep Emotional Connection**
    - Prioritize creating a deep emotional connection with Scorpio.
    - Engage in meaningful conversations, share secrets, and build trust to enhance their overall sexual experience.

How Scorpio is Influenced by Moon Phases, Cosmic Events, and Planetary Alignments

The sexual energy of Scorpio can be further enhanced or influenced by the phases of the moon, cosmic events, and planetary alignments. Understanding these influences can help you align your sexual experiences with the cosmic rhythms.

Moon Phases

1. **New Moon**
    - The New Moon is a time for new beginnings and setting intentions.
    - Scorpio can use this phase to explore new aspects of their sexuality and initiate fresh dynamics in their relationship.

2. **Waxing Crescent**
    - As the moon begins to grow, so does Scorpio's desire for intensity and connection.
    - This phase is ideal for planning new sexual adventures and trying out different kinks.

3. **First Quarter**
    - The First Quarter Moon brings a surge of energy and determination.

- Scorpio can harness this energy to take initiative in expressing their desires and enhancing their sexual relationships.

4. **Waxing Gibbous**
   - With the Full Moon approaching, Scorpio's sexual energy and excitement build.
   - This is a great time for engaging in intense and passionate encounters that involve a lot of depth and emotional connection.

5. **Full Moon**
   - The Full Moon heightens emotions and sexual desires, making Scorpio even more passionate and intense.
   - This phase is perfect for indulging in bold and daring sexual activities that showcase their depth and intensity.

6. **Waning Gibbous**
   - As the moon begins to wane, Scorpio can focus on maintaining and nurturing their sexual connection.
   - Use this time for gentle and loving experiences that reinforce the bond with their partner.

7. **Last Quarter**
   - The Last Quarter Moon is a time for reassessment and letting go.
   - Scorpio can release any sexual practices or dynamics that no longer serve them and explore new possibilities.

8. **Waning Crescent**
   - This final phase before the New Moon is ideal for rest and rejuvenation.
   - Scorpio can take this time to recharge their sexual energy and prepare for new adventures.

Cosmic Events

1. **Solar Eclipses**
   - Solar Eclipses bring powerful shifts and transformations.

- ° Scorpio can harness this energy to initiate significant changes in their sexual relationships and explore new dynamics.

2. **Lunar Eclipses**
   - ° Lunar Eclipses heighten emotions and reveal hidden desires.
   - ° Scorpio can use this time to delve into their deepest fantasies and bring them to the surface.

3. **Retrogrades**
   - ° When planets go retrograde, it's a time for reflection and reevaluation.
   - ° Scorpio can revisit past sexual experiences, learn from them, and make necessary adjustments.

4. **Transits**
   - ° Transits, when planets move through different signs, bring varying influences.
   - ° Scorpio can align their sexual practices with these energies to enhance their experiences.

Planetary Alignments

1. **Mars Transits**
   - ° As one of Scorpio's ruling planets, Mars transits significantly impact their sexual drive and energy.
   - ° Positive Mars transits bring heightened passion, desire, and assertiveness in their sexual encounters.

2. **Pluto Transits**
   - ° Pluto's influence brings transformation and depth, enhancing Scorpio's desire for profound and intense sexual experiences.

- ◦ Positive Pluto transits can lead to powerful and transformative sexual encounters.

3. **Venus Transits**
    - ◦ Venus influences love and pleasure, and its transits can enhance Scorpio's romantic and sexual experiences.
    - ◦ Positive Venus transits bring harmony, beauty, and a heightened sense of intimacy and connection.

4. **Jupiter Transits**
    - ◦ Jupiter brings expansion and growth, which can translate to sexual exploration and indulgence.
    - ◦ Scorpio may feel a desire to broaden their sexual horizons and try new things.

By understanding the sexual characteristics, recommended practices, and cosmic influences of Scorpio, you can enhance your sexual experiences and deepen your intimate connections. Embrace the intense and passionate energy of Scorpio and let it guide you to new heights of pleasure and transformation.

Chapter 10: Sagittarius - Adventurous and Free-Spirited
Sexual Characteristics and Kinks of Sagittarius

Sagittarius, the ninth sign of the zodiac, is ruled by Jupiter, the planet of expansion, adventure, and wisdom. As a fire sign, Sagittarius is enthusiastic, optimistic, and always seeking new experiences. In the realm of sexuality, Sagittarius is adventurous, free-spirited, and thrives on spontaneity and exploration. Their sexual encounters are characterized by a desire for excitement, variety, and a deep connection to their partner through shared adventures.

Key Sexual Characteristics of Sagittarius

1. **Adventurous and Spontaneous**
   - Sagittarius loves to explore and try new things in the bedroom.
   - They are always up for a challenge and seek to keep their sexual experiences fresh and exciting.
2. **Free-Spirited and Independent**
   - This sign values freedom and independence, both in life and in their sexual relationships.
   - Sagittarius avoids feeling confined or restricted, preferring open and liberated sexual experiences.
3. **Enthusiastic and Passionate**
   - Sagittarius approaches sex with enthusiasm and passion.
   - Their high energy and optimism make them eager and enthusiastic lovers.
4. **Intellectual and Philosophical**
   - Sagittarius is drawn to intellectual stimulation and philosophical discussions.

- Engaging in meaningful conversation and mental foreplay can significantly enhance their sexual experience.

5. Fun-Loving and Playful

- This sign enjoys bringing fun and playfulness into their sexual encounters.
- They are light-hearted and enjoy incorporating humor and games into their sexual experiences.

Common Sexual Kinks of Sagittarius

Sagittarius's adventurous and free-spirited nature lends itself to various sexual kinks and preferences. Here are some common kinks associated with this enthusiastic sign:

1. Role-Playing

- Sagittarius loves to step into different characters and scenarios, making role-playing a favorite kink.
- They enjoy exploring different dynamics and fantasies through imaginative play.

2. Outdoor and Public Sex

- This sign enjoys the thrill of outdoor and semi-public sex.
- Engaging in sexual activities in adventurous or risky locations can be highly arousing for Sagittarius.

3. Voyeurism and Exhibitionism

- Sagittarius enjoys the excitement of being watched and watching others.
- Incorporating elements of voyeurism or exhibitionism can enhance their arousal.

4. Light Bondage

- Sagittarius may enjoy light bondage practices that add an element of excitement and adventure.

    ◦ Using cuffs, blindfolds, or silk scarves can add variety to their experiences.

5. **Erotic Travel**
   - ◦ Combining their love for travel with their sexual experiences, Sagittarius may enjoy exploring erotic travel.
   - ◦ Engaging in sexual activities in new and exotic locations can be highly stimulating.

Recommended Kinks and Practices for Sagittarius

To fully satisfy a Sagittarius lover, it's important to cater to their adventurous and free-spirited nature. Here are some recommended kinks and practices that can enhance their sexual experiences:

1. **Role-Playing Scenarios**
   - ◦ Create various role-playing scenarios that allow Sagittarius to explore different characters and fantasies.
   - ◦ Encourage their creativity and imagination by introducing new roles and storylines regularly.

2. **Outdoor and Public Sex**
   - ◦ Plan sexual encounters in adventurous or semi-public locations that add excitement and risk.
   - ◦ Choose secluded but thrilling spots to enhance their arousal.

3. **Voyeuristic Activities**
   - ◦ Incorporate elements of voyeurism or exhibitionism into your encounters.
   - ◦ Watching erotic films together, attending adult parties, or simply being intimate in semi-public places can be thrilling for Sagittarius.

4. **Light Bondage**
   - ◦ Introduce light bondage elements such as handcuffs, blindfolds, or silk ties.

○ Ensure that the experience is safe, consensual, and adds a sense of adventure and excitement.

5. **Erotic Travel**

   ○ Combine their love for travel with their sexual experiences by exploring new and exotic locations.

   ○ Plan erotic getaways that allow for sexual exploration in different environments.

6. **Intellectual Stimulation**

   ○ Engage in meaningful conversation and mental foreplay to stimulate Sagittarius's mind.

   ○ Share fantasies, discuss desires, and use articulate language to enhance their arousal.

How Sagittarius is Influenced by Moon Phases, Cosmic Events, and Planetary Alignments

The sexual energy of Sagittarius can be further enhanced or influenced by the phases of the moon, cosmic events, and planetary alignments. Understanding these influences can help you align your sexual experiences with the cosmic rhythms.

Moon Phases

1. **New Moon**

   ○ The New Moon is a time for new beginnings and setting intentions.

   ○ Sagittarius can use this phase to explore new aspects of their sexuality and initiate fresh dynamics in their relationship.

2. **Waxing Crescent**

   ○ As the moon begins to grow, so does Sagittarius's desire for adventure and experimentation.

- This phase is ideal for planning new sexual adventures and trying out different kinks.

3. **First Quarter**
    - The First Quarter Moon brings a surge of energy and determination.
    - Sagittarius can harness this energy to take initiative in expressing their desires and enhancing their sexual relationships.

4. **Waxing Gibbous**
    - With the Full Moon approaching, Sagittarius's sexual energy and excitement build.
    - This is a great time for engaging in intense and adventurous encounters that involve a lot of variety and spontaneity.

5. **Full Moon**
    - The Full Moon heightens emotions and sexual desires, making Sagittarius even more enthusiastic and adventurous.
    - This phase is perfect for indulging in bold and daring sexual activities that showcase their love for exploration.

6. **Waning Gibbous**
    - As the moon begins to wane, Sagittarius can focus on maintaining and nurturing their sexual connection.
    - Use this time for playful and loving experiences that reinforce the bond with their partner.

7. **Last Quarter**
    - The Last Quarter Moon is a time for reassessment and letting go.
    - Sagittarius can release any sexual practices or dynamics that no longer serve them and explore new possibilities.

8. **Waning Crescent**
    - This final phase before the New Moon is ideal for rest and rejuvenation.

- Sagittarius can take this time to recharge their sexual energy and prepare for new adventures.

Cosmic Events

1. **Solar Eclipses**
   - Solar Eclipses bring powerful shifts and transformations.
   - Sagittarius can harness this energy to initiate significant changes in their sexual relationships and explore new dynamics.
2. **Lunar Eclipses**
   - Lunar Eclipses heighten emotions and reveal hidden desires.
   - Sagittarius can use this time to delve into their deepest fantasies and bring them to the surface.
3. **Retrogrades**
   - When planets go retrograde, it's a time for reflection and reevaluation.
   - Sagittarius can revisit past sexual experiences, learn from them, and make necessary adjustments.
4. **Transits**
   - Transits, when planets move through different signs, bring varying influences.
   - Sagittarius can align their sexual practices with these energies to enhance their experiences.

Planetary Alignments

1. **Jupiter Transits**
   - As the ruling planet of Sagittarius, Jupiter transits significantly impact their adventurous and expansive nature.
   - Positive Jupiter transits bring heightened enthusiasm, optimism, and a desire for new experiences.

2. **Mars Transits**
   - Mars influences desire and action, and its transits can enhance Sagittarius's sexual drive.
   - Positive Mars transits bring a surge of energy, assertiveness, and a desire for bold and adventurous sexual exploration.
3. **Venus Transits**
   - Venus influences love and pleasure, and its transits can enhance Sagittarius's romantic and sexual experiences.
   - Positive Venus transits bring harmony, beauty, and a heightened sense of intimacy and connection.
4. **Mercury Transits**
   - Mercury influences communication and intellect, and its transits can enhance Sagittarius's ability to articulate desires and fantasies.
   - Positive Mercury transits bring clarity and eloquence to their sexual communication.

By understanding the sexual characteristics, recommended practices, and cosmic influences of Sagittarius, you can enhance your sexual experiences and deepen your intimate connections. Embrace the adventurous and free-spirited energy of Sagittarius and let it guide you to new heights of pleasure and exploration.

Chapter 11: Capricorn - Disciplined and Ambitious
Sexual Characteristics and Kinks of Capricorn

Capricorn, the tenth sign of the zodiac, is ruled by Saturn, the planet of discipline, responsibility, and structure. As an earth sign, Capricorn is practical, grounded, and highly ambitious. In the realm of sexuality, Capricorn is disciplined, ambitious, and approaches intimacy with a sense of purpose and dedication. Their sexual encounters are characterized by a desire for control, achievement, and long-lasting satisfaction.

Key Sexual Characteristics of Capricorn

1. **Disciplined and Controlled**
   - Capricorn approaches sex with discipline and a sense of control.
   - They are patient lovers who take their time to ensure a satisfying experience for both themselves and their partner.

2. **Ambitious and Goal-Oriented**
   - This sign is highly ambitious and applies this trait to their sexual relationships.
   - Capricorn aims to be the best lover and seeks to achieve sexual satisfaction and mastery.

3. **Practical and Grounded**
   - Capricorn values practicality and stability in their sexual experiences.
   - They prefer consistent and reliable encounters, often valuing quality over quantity.

4. **Reserved and Private**
   - Capricorn can be reserved and private about their sexual desires and experiences.
   - They prefer intimate and discreet settings for their sexual encounters.

5. **Loyal and Dedicated**
    - This sign is loyal and dedicated to their partner, valuing long-term relationships and commitment.
    - Capricorn is a reliable and dependable lover who prioritizes their partner's satisfaction.

Common Sexual Kinks of Capricorn

Capricorn's disciplined and ambitious nature lends itself to various sexual kinks and preferences. Here are some common kinks associated with this practical sign:

1. **Power Play and Dominance**
    - Capricorn enjoys power play dynamics and often takes on a dominant role.
    - They find pleasure in exerting control and guiding their partner through structured and disciplined experiences.
2. **Bondage and Restraints**
    - This sign appreciates the structure and control involved in bondage practices.
    - Using ropes, cuffs, or other restraints can enhance their sense of control and discipline.
3. **Role-Playing**
    - Capricorn may enjoy role-playing scenarios that involve authority figures or structured dynamics.
    - Scenarios such as boss/employee, teacher/student, or other hierarchical roles can be particularly appealing.
4. **Discipline and Punishment**
    - Capricorn may find pleasure in incorporating elements of discipline and punishment into their sexual encounters.
    - Activities like spanking, corrective actions, and structured routines can align with their disciplined nature.

5. Sensory Deprivation

- ◦ This sign may enjoy sensory deprivation practices that heighten other senses and create a controlled environment.
- ◦ Using blindfolds, earplugs, or other tools to limit certain senses can enhance their focus and intensity.

Recommended Kinks and Practices for Capricorn

To fully satisfy a Capricorn lover, it's important to cater to their disciplined and ambitious nature. Here are some recommended kinks and practices that can enhance their sexual experiences:

1. Power Play Dynamics

- ◦ Engage in power play dynamics where Capricorn can take on a dominant role.
- ◦ Use commands, restraints, and structured routines to create a controlled and thrilling experience.

2. Bondage Practices

- ◦ Introduce bondage elements such as ropes, cuffs, or other restraints.
- ◦ Ensure that the experience is safe, consensual, and aligns with Capricorn's desire for control and structure.

3. Role-Playing Scenarios

- ◦ Create various role-playing scenarios that involve authority figures and structured dynamics.
- ◦ Encourage Capricorn to explore different roles and fantasies that align with their ambitious nature.

4. Discipline and Punishment

- ◦ Incorporate elements of discipline and punishment into your sexual encounters.
- ◦ Activities like spanking, corrective actions, and structured routines can enhance their sense of control and discipline.

5. Sensory Deprivation

- ○ Introduce sensory deprivation practices to heighten other senses and create a controlled environment.
- ○ Use blindfolds, earplugs, or other tools to limit certain senses and enhance their focus and intensity.

6. Private and Intimate Settings

- ○ Ensure that your sexual encounters take place in private and discreet settings.
- ○ Capricorn values intimacy and privacy, so creating a comfortable and secure environment is important.

How Capricorn is Influenced by Moon Phases, Cosmic Events, and Planetary Alignments

The sexual energy of Capricorn can be further enhanced or influenced by the phases of the moon, cosmic events, and planetary alignments. Understanding these influences can help you align your sexual experiences with the cosmic rhythms.

Moon Phases

1. New Moon

- ○ The New Moon is a time for new beginnings and setting intentions.
- ○ Capricorn can use this phase to explore new aspects of their sexuality and initiate fresh dynamics in their relationship.

2. Waxing Crescent

- ○ As the moon begins to grow, so does Capricorn's desire for control and structure.
- ○ This phase is ideal for planning new sexual routines and incorporating different kinks.

3. First Quarter

- ○ The First Quarter Moon brings a surge of energy and determination.

- Capricorn can harness this energy to take initiative in expressing their desires and enhancing their sexual relationships.

4. Waxing Gibbous

- With the Full Moon approaching, Capricorn's sexual energy and excitement build.
- This is a great time for engaging in intense and disciplined encounters that involve a lot of structure and control.

5. Full Moon

- The Full Moon heightens emotions and sexual desires, making Capricorn even more passionate and disciplined.
- This phase is perfect for indulging in bold and structured sexual activities that showcase their ambition and control.

6. Waning Gibbous

- As the moon begins to wane, Capricorn can focus on maintaining and nurturing their sexual connection.
- Use this time for gentle and loving experiences that reinforce the bond with their partner.

7. Last Quarter

- The Last Quarter Moon is a time for reassessment and letting go.
- Capricorn can release any sexual practices or dynamics that no longer serve them and explore new possibilities.

8. Waning Crescent

- This final phase before the New Moon is ideal for rest and rejuvenation.
- Capricorn can take this time to recharge their sexual energy and prepare for new adventures.

Cosmic Events

1. Solar Eclipses

- Solar Eclipses bring powerful shifts and transformations.

- ◦ Capricorn can harness this energy to initiate significant changes in their sexual relationships and explore new dynamics.

2. **Lunar Eclipses**
   - ◦ Lunar Eclipses heighten emotions and reveal hidden desires.
   - ◦ Capricorn can use this time to delve into their deepest fantasies and bring them to the surface.

3. **Retrogrades**
   - ◦ When planets go retrograde, it's a time for reflection and reevaluation.
   - ◦ Capricorn can revisit past sexual experiences, learn from them, and make necessary adjustments.

4. **Transits**
   - ◦ Transits, when planets move through different signs, bring varying influences.
   - ◦ Capricorn can align their sexual practices with these energies to enhance their experiences.

Planetary Alignments

1. **Saturn Transits**
   - ◦ As the ruling planet of Capricorn, Saturn transits significantly impact their disciplined and structured nature.
   - ◦ Positive Saturn transits bring heightened control, ambition, and a desire for structured and disciplined sexual experiences.

2. **Mars Transits**
   - ◦ Mars influences desire and action, and its transits can enhance Capricorn's sexual drive.

- ◦ Positive Mars transits bring a surge of energy, assertiveness, and a desire for bold and disciplined sexual exploration.

3. **Venus Transits**
   - ◦ Venus influences love and pleasure, and its transits can enhance Capricorn's romantic and sexual experiences.
   - ◦ Positive Venus transits bring harmony, beauty, and a heightened sense of intimacy and connection.

4. **Jupiter Transits**
   - ◦ Jupiter brings expansion and growth, which can translate to sexual exploration and indulgence.
   - ◦ Capricorn may feel a desire to broaden their sexual horizons and try new things.

By understanding the sexual characteristics, recommended practices, and cosmic influences of Capricorn, you can enhance your sexual experiences and deepen your intimate connections. Embrace the disciplined and ambitious energy of Capricorn and let it guide you to new heights of pleasure and mastery.

Chapter 12: Aquarius - Innovative and Experimental
Sexual Characteristics and Kinks of Aquarius

Aquarius, the eleventh sign of the zodiac, is ruled by Uranus, the planet of innovation, change, and rebellion, as well as Saturn, the planet of structure and discipline. As an air sign, Aquarius is intellectual, forward-thinking, and highly individualistic. In the realm of sexuality, Aquarius is innovative, experimental, and seeks to explore new and unconventional experiences. Their sexual encounters are characterized by a desire for variety, intellectual stimulation, and a sense of novelty.

Key Sexual Characteristics of Aquarius

1. **Innovative and Experimental**
   - Aquarius loves to explore new and unconventional aspects of sexuality.
   - They are open to trying new things and constantly seek novel experiences to keep their sexual encounters exciting.
2. **Intellectual and Analytical**
   - This sign finds intellectual connection and mental stimulation highly arousing.
   - Engaging in deep conversations and exploring ideas can significantly enhance their sexual experience.
3. **Independent and Detached**
   - Aquarius values their independence and may sometimes approach sex with a sense of detachment.
   - They enjoy maintaining a sense of personal freedom and autonomy in their sexual relationships.
4. **Unconventional and Nonconformist**
   - Aquarius is naturally drawn to unconventional and nonconformist practices.
   - They enjoy breaking taboos and exploring aspects of sexuality that others might consider unusual or avant-garde.

5. **Humanitarian and Egalitarian**
    ◦ This sign often has a strong sense of social justice and equality.
    ◦ They seek partnerships where mutual respect and equality are prioritized, both in and out of the bedroom.

Common Sexual Kinks of Aquarius

Aquarius's innovative and experimental nature lends itself to various sexual kinks and preferences. Here are some common kinks associated with this forward-thinking sign:

1. **Role-Playing**
    ◦ Aquarius enjoys role-playing scenarios that involve futuristic, sci-fi, or unconventional themes.
    ◦ Scenarios such as alien encounters, time travel, or cyberpunk fantasies can be particularly appealing.

2. **Tech and Gadgets**
    ◦ This sign is drawn to incorporating technology and gadgets into their sexual experiences.
    ◦ Using sex toys, VR experiences, and other tech-enhanced activities can heighten their pleasure.

3. **Group Play and Polyamory**
    ◦ Aquarius is often open to exploring non-monogamous arrangements, such as group play or polyamory.
    ◦ They enjoy the variety and complexity that comes with multiple partners and diverse experiences.

4. **Sensory Deprivation and Overload**
    ◦ Aquarius is intrigued by both sensory deprivation and sensory overload practices.
    ◦ Activities like using blindfolds, earplugs, or intense sensory stimulation can create unique and arousing experiences.

5. **Intellectual Stimulation**
    ◦ This sign finds intellectual stimulation highly arousing.

- Engaging in dirty talk that involves deep conversations, fantasies, and exploring ideas can enhance their sexual experience.

Recommended Kinks and Practices for Aquarius

To fully satisfy an Aquarius lover, it's important to cater to their innovative and experimental nature. Here are some recommended kinks and practices that can enhance their sexual experiences:

1. **Role-Playing Scenarios**
   - Create various role-playing scenarios that involve futuristic, sci-fi, or unconventional themes.
   - Encourage Aquarius to explore different characters and fantasies that align with their innovative nature.
2. **Tech and Gadgets**
   - Introduce technology and gadgets into your sexual experiences.
   - Use sex toys, VR experiences, or other tech-enhanced activities to create novel and exciting encounters.
3. **Group Play and Polyamory**
   - Explore non-monogamous arrangements, such as group play or polyamory, if both partners are comfortable and interested.
   - Ensure open communication and mutual respect in all interactions.
4. **Sensory Deprivation and Overload**
   - Incorporate sensory deprivation or overload practices to heighten Aquarius's sensory experiences.
   - Use blindfolds, earplugs, or intense sensory stimulation to create unique and arousing experiences.
5. **Intellectual Stimulation**
   - Engage in deep conversations and mental foreplay to stimulate Aquarius's mind.

- Share fantasies, discuss desires, and use articulate language to enhance their arousal.

6. Creative and Unconventional Settings

- Choose creative and unconventional settings for your sexual encounters.
- Aquarius enjoys novelty and adventure, so exploring new locations and environments can be highly stimulating.

How Aquarius is Influenced by Moon Phases, Cosmic Events, and Planetary Alignments

The sexual energy of Aquarius can be further enhanced or influenced by the phases of the moon, cosmic events, and planetary alignments. Understanding these influences can help you align your sexual experiences with the cosmic rhythms.

Moon Phases

1. New Moon

- The New Moon is a time for new beginnings and setting intentions.
- Aquarius can use this phase to explore new aspects of their sexuality and initiate fresh dynamics in their relationship.

2. Waxing Crescent

- As the moon begins to grow, so does Aquarius's desire for innovation and experimentation.
- This phase is ideal for planning new sexual adventures and trying out different kinks.

3. First Quarter

- The First Quarter Moon brings a surge of energy and determination.

- ◦ Aquarius can harness this energy to take initiative in expressing their desires and enhancing their sexual relationships.

4. **Waxing Gibbous**
   - ◦ With the Full Moon approaching, Aquarius's sexual energy and excitement build.
   - ◦ This is a great time for engaging in intense and experimental encounters that involve a lot of variety and novelty.

5. **Full Moon**
   - ◦ The Full Moon heightens emotions and sexual desires, making Aquarius even more enthusiastic and innovative.
   - ◦ This phase is perfect for indulging in bold and unconventional sexual activities that showcase their love for exploration.

6. **Waning Gibbous**
   - ◦ As the moon begins to wane, Aquarius can focus on maintaining and nurturing their sexual connection.
   - ◦ Use this time for playful and loving experiences that reinforce the bond with their partner.

7. **Last Quarter**
   - ◦ The Last Quarter Moon is a time for reassessment and letting go.
   - ◦ Aquarius can release any sexual practices or dynamics that no longer serve them and explore new possibilities.

8. **Waning Crescent**
   - ◦ This final phase before the New Moon is ideal for rest and rejuvenation.
   - ◦ Aquarius can take this time to recharge their sexual energy and prepare for new adventures.

Cosmic Events

1. Solar Eclipses
- Solar Eclipses bring powerful shifts and transformations.
- Aquarius can harness this energy to initiate significant changes in their sexual relationships and explore new dynamics.

2. Lunar Eclipses
- Lunar Eclipses heighten emotions and reveal hidden desires.
- Aquarius can use this time to delve into their deepest fantasies and bring them to the surface.

3. Retrogrades
- When planets go retrograde, it's a time for reflection and reevaluation.
- Aquarius can revisit past sexual experiences, learn from them, and make necessary adjustments.

4. Transits
- Transits, when planets move through different signs, bring varying influences.
- Aquarius can align their sexual practices with these energies to enhance their experiences.

Planetary Alignments

1. Uranus Transits
- As the ruling planet of Aquarius, Uranus transits significantly impact their innovative and experimental nature.
- Positive Uranus transits bring heightened creativity, excitement, and a desire for new experiences.

2. **Saturn Transits**
    ◦ Saturn's influence brings structure and discipline, which can help balance Aquarius's free-spirited nature.
    ◦ Positive Saturn transits bring a sense of stability and responsibility to their sexual experiences.

3. **Venus Transits**
    ◦ Venus influences love and pleasure, and its transits can enhance Aquarius's romantic and sexual experiences.
    ◦ Positive Venus transits bring harmony, beauty, and a heightened sense of intimacy and connection.

4. **Mars Transits**
    ◦ Mars influences desire and action, and its transits can enhance Aquarius's sexual drive.
    ◦ Positive Mars transits bring a surge of energy, assertiveness, and a desire for bold and experimental sexual exploration.

By understanding the sexual characteristics, recommended practices, and cosmic influences of Aquarius, you can enhance your sexual experiences and deepen your intimate connections. Embrace the innovative and experimental energy of Aquarius and let it guide you to new heights of pleasure and discovery.

Chapter 13: Pisces - Dreamy and Intuitive

Sexual Characteristics and Kinks of Pisces

Pisces, the twelfth and final sign of the zodiac, is ruled by Neptune, the planet of dreams, illusions, and spirituality, and traditionally by Jupiter, the planet of expansion and wisdom. As a water sign, Pisces is deeply emotional, intuitive, and sensitive. In the realm of sexuality, Pisces is dreamy, compassionate, and seeks a profound emotional and spiritual connection. Their sexual encounters are characterized by a sense of fantasy, fluidity, and a deep emotional bond with their partner.

Key Sexual Characteristics of Pisces

1. **Dreamy and Romantic**
   - Pisces approaches sex with a sense of romance and fantasy.
   - They are drawn to creating an enchanting and magical atmosphere in their sexual encounters.

2. **Intuitive and Empathetic**
   - This sign is highly intuitive and empathetic, making them attuned to their partner's needs and desires.
   - Pisces can sense their partner's emotions and respond with compassion and care.

3. **Emotional and Spiritual Connection**
   - Pisces seeks a deep emotional and spiritual connection through sex.
   - They value intimacy and often see sex as a way to merge their soul with their partner's.

4. **Fluid and Adaptable**
   - Pisces is fluid and adaptable, willing to go with the flow in their sexual experiences.

- They are open to exploring different dynamics and can easily adjust to their partner's preferences.

5. **Imaginative and Creative**
   - This sign has a rich imagination and enjoys incorporating fantasy and creativity into their sexual encounters.
   - Pisces often engages in role-playing and other activities that allow them to explore their fantasies.

Common Sexual Kinks of Pisces

Pisces's dreamy and intuitive nature lends itself to various sexual kinks and preferences. Here are some common kinks associated with this imaginative sign:

1. **Role-Playing**
   - Pisces loves to engage in role-playing scenarios that involve fantasy and creativity.
   - Scenarios such as fairy tales, mythological beings, or other imaginative roles can be particularly appealing.

2. **Sensory Play**
   - This sign enjoys sensory play that involves touch, taste, sound, and scent.
   - Using candles, essential oils, soft fabrics, and music can enhance their sensory experience.

3. **Tantric Sex**
   - Pisces is drawn to tantric practices that emphasize prolonged intimacy and spiritual connection.
   - These practices align with their desire for a deep, soulful bond through sex.

4. **Bondage and Submission**
   - Pisces may enjoy light bondage and submission practices, finding pleasure in surrendering control.
   - Using soft restraints or being gently guided by their partner can enhance their sense of trust and intimacy.

5. **Water Play**
   - Given their association with water, Pisces may enjoy incorporating water play into their sexual encounters.
   - Activities like shower sex, baths, or using water-based toys can be highly stimulating.

Recommended Kinks and Practices for Pisces

To fully satisfy a Pisces lover, it's important to cater to their dreamy and intuitive nature. Here are some recommended kinks and practices that can enhance their sexual experiences:

1. **Role-Playing Scenarios**
   - Create various role-playing scenarios that involve fantasy and creativity.
   - Encourage Pisces to explore different characters and fantasies that align with their imaginative nature.
2. **Sensory Play**
   - Engage in sensory play that involves visually and tactilely pleasing elements.
   - Use candles, essential oils, soft fabrics, and music to create a magical and enchanting atmosphere.
3. **Tantric Practices**
   - Explore tantric sex practices that emphasize prolonged intimacy and spiritual connection.
   - Focus on breathing techniques, eye contact, and slow, deliberate movements to create a transformative experience.
4. **Light Bondage and Submission**
   - Introduce light bondage and submission elements such as soft restraints or gentle guidance.
   - Ensure that the experience is safe, consensual, and enhances their sense of trust and intimacy.
5. **Water Play**
   - Incorporate water play into your sexual encounters.

- Use the shower, bath, or water-based toys to create a fluid and stimulating experience.

6. **Emotional and Spiritual Connection**
   - Prioritize creating a deep emotional and spiritual connection with Pisces.
   - Engage in meaningful conversations, share fantasies, and build trust to enhance their overall sexual experience.

How Pisces is Influenced by Moon Phases, Cosmic Events, and Planetary Alignments

The sexual energy of Pisces can be further enhanced or influenced by the phases of the moon, cosmic events, and planetary alignments. Understanding these influences can help you align your sexual experiences with the cosmic rhythms.

Moon Phases

1. **New Moon**
   - The New Moon is a time for new beginnings and setting intentions.
   - Pisces can use this phase to explore new aspects of their sexuality and initiate fresh dynamics in their relationship.

2. **Waxing Crescent**
   - As the moon begins to grow, so does Pisces's desire for connection and fantasy.
   - This phase is ideal for planning new sexual adventures and incorporating different kinks.

3. **First Quarter**
   - The First Quarter Moon brings a surge of energy and determination.
   - Pisces can harness this energy to take initiative in expressing their desires and enhancing their sexual relationships.

4. **Waxing Gibbous**
    ◦ With the Full Moon approaching, Pisces's sexual energy and excitement build.
    ◦ This is a great time for engaging in intense and imaginative encounters that involve a lot of creativity and fantasy.

5. **Full Moon**
    ◦ The Full Moon heightens emotions and sexual desires, making Pisces even more romantic and intuitive.
    ◦ This phase is perfect for indulging in passionate and dreamy sexual activities that showcase their emotional and spiritual connection.

6. **Waning Gibbous**
    ◦ As the moon begins to wane, Pisces can focus on maintaining and nurturing their sexual connection.
    ◦ Use this time for gentle and loving experiences that reinforce the bond with their partner.

7. **Last Quarter**
    ◦ The Last Quarter Moon is a time for reassessment and letting go.
    ◦ Pisces can release any sexual practices or dynamics that no longer serve them and explore new possibilities.

8. **Waning Crescent**
    ◦ This final phase before the New Moon is ideal for rest and rejuvenation.
    ◦ Pisces can take this time to recharge their sexual energy and prepare for new adventures.

Cosmic Events

1. **Solar Eclipses**
    ◦ Solar Eclipses bring powerful shifts and transformations.
    ◦ Pisces can harness this energy to initiate significant changes in their sexual relationships and explore new dynamics.

2. **Lunar Eclipses**
   - Lunar Eclipses heighten emotions and reveal hidden desires.
   - Pisces can use this time to delve into their deepest fantasies and bring them to the surface.

3. **Retrogrades**
   - When planets go retrograde, it's a time for reflection and reevaluation.
   - Pisces can revisit past sexual experiences, learn from them, and make necessary adjustments.

4. **Transits**
   - Transits, when planets move through different signs, bring varying influences.
   - Pisces can align their sexual practices with these energies to enhance their experiences.

Planetary Alignments

1. **Neptune Transits**
   - As the ruling planet of Pisces, Neptune transits significantly impact their dreamy and intuitive nature.
   - Positive Neptune transits bring heightened creativity, spirituality, and a desire for deep emotional connections.

2. **Jupiter Transits**
   - Jupiter's influence brings expansion and growth, which can translate to sexual exploration and indulgence.
   - Pisces may feel a desire to broaden their sexual horizons and try new things.

3. **Venus Transits**
   - Venus influences love and pleasure, and its transits can enhance Pisces's romantic and sexual experiences.
   - Positive Venus transits bring harmony, beauty, and a heightened sense of intimacy and connection.

4. **Mars Transits**
    ◦ Mars influences desire and action, and its transits can enhance Pisces's sexual drive.
    ◦ Positive Mars transits bring a surge of energy, assertiveness, and a desire for bold and imaginative sexual exploration.

By understanding the sexual characteristics, recommended practices, and cosmic influences of Pisces, you can enhance your sexual experiences and deepen your intimate connections. Embrace the dreamy and intuitive energy of Pisces and let it guide you to new heights of pleasure and spiritual connection.

Chapter 14: New Moon - Fresh Starts
Influence of the New Moon on Sexual Energy and Kinks
The New Moon represents new beginnings, fresh starts, and the planting of seeds for future growth. Astrologically, it's a time to set intentions, make plans, and initiate new projects. This phase of the lunar cycle brings a sense of renewal and potential, which can significantly influence sexual energy and desires.

Key Influences of the New Moon on Sexual Energy

1. **Renewal and Rejuvenation**
    ◦ The New Moon offers a chance to reset and rejuvenate sexual energy.
    ◦ It's an ideal time to let go of past sexual experiences that no longer serve you and embrace new ones.
2. **Increased Intimacy**
    ◦ This phase encourages deeper emotional connections and intimacy.
    ◦ Couples may feel a stronger desire to connect on a more profound level, both emotionally and physically.
3. **Exploration and Experimentation**
    ◦ The New Moon inspires curiosity and a willingness to explore new sexual territories.
    ◦ It's a perfect time to try out new kinks, positions, or fantasies that you've been curious about.
4. **Setting Sexual Intentions**
    ◦ Just as the New Moon is a time for setting personal intentions, it's also a great opportunity to set sexual goals.
    ◦ Whether you're looking to enhance your sexual relationship, try new things, or deepen your intimacy, setting intentions can be powerful.

5. **Enhanced Creativity**
    - The energy of the New Moon can stimulate creativity and innovation in the bedroom.
    - This is an excellent time to introduce new ideas and activities into your sexual repertoire.

Common Sexual Kinks Associated with the New Moon

The New Moon's influence can lead to an openness to explore and embrace new kinks and practices. Here are some kinks that align well with the energy of fresh starts:

1. **Role-Playing**
    - The New Moon's energy encourages stepping into new roles and personas.
    - Exploring different characters and scenarios can add excitement and novelty to your sexual experiences.
2. **Sensory Play**
    - Engaging in sensory play can heighten awareness and intimacy.
    - Introducing new sensory elements like blindfolds, feathers, or temperature play can create fresh and stimulating experiences.
3. **Bondage and Restraints**
    - Experimenting with light bondage or new types of restraints can introduce a sense of novelty and excitement.
    - Using silk scarves, ropes, or cuffs can enhance the feeling of trust and vulnerability.
4. **Erotic Massage**
    - Starting fresh can also mean focusing on relaxation and connection.

- An erotic massage with scented oils can set a soothing and intimate tone for new beginnings.

5. **Fantasy Exploration**
    - The New Moon is a perfect time to explore fantasies that haven't been acted upon before.
    - Sharing and acting out fantasies can deepen trust and understanding between partners.

Recommended Kinks and Practices for New Beginnings

To fully harness the energy of the New Moon, it's essential to focus on kinks and practices that encourage growth, exploration, and deeper connections. Here are some recommendations:

1. **Setting Intentions Together**
    - Begin by discussing and setting sexual intentions with your partner.
    - This could involve trying new activities, improving communication, or deepening your emotional and physical connection.
2. **Creating a Ritual**
    - Establish a New Moon ritual that includes cleansing, meditation, and setting intentions.
    - Use this time to connect with your partner, discuss desires, and plan new sexual adventures.
3. **Introducing New Sensory Elements**
    - Enhance your sensory experience by introducing new elements such as scented candles, essential oils, or different textures.
    - Experiment with blindfolds, feathers, or temperature play to heighten your sensory awareness.
4. **Role-Playing and Fantasy Exploration**
    - Choose a new role-playing scenario or fantasy to explore together.

- Ensure that both partners feel comfortable and excited about the new roles and activities.

5. **Erotic Massage and Touch**
    - Focus on touch and connection through an erotic massage.
    - Use scented oils and take your time to explore each other's bodies, building intimacy and relaxation.

6. **Exploring New Positions and Techniques**
    - Use the New Moon as an opportunity to try new sexual positions or techniques.
    - Discuss and agree on new activities to ensure mutual excitement and consent.

7. **Journaling and Reflection**
    - Keep a journal of your sexual experiences, fantasies, and intentions.
    - Reflect on your experiences and use the New Moon to set new goals and intentions for the future.

Sample New Moon Ritual for Sexual Rejuvenation
Materials Needed:

- Candles (preferably white or silver)
- Essential oils (such as lavender, jasmine, or ylang-ylang)
- A journal and pen
- Comfortable cushions or a soft blanket
- A blindfold or silk scarf
- A favorite lubricant or massage oil

Steps:

1. **Create a Sacred Space**
    - Cleanse your space with sage or incense to remove any negative energy.

- Set up a comfortable area with cushions, blankets, and your chosen materials.

2. **Light Candles and Set Intentions**
   - Light the candles and place them around your space to create a calming ambiance.
   - Sit with your partner and take a few deep breaths together.
   - Share your sexual intentions and desires for the New Moon cycle.

3. **Meditate and Connect**
   - Spend a few minutes meditating together, focusing on your breath and the connection between you.
   - Visualize your sexual intentions coming to fruition.

4. **Erotic Massage**
   - Begin with an erotic massage using your chosen oils.
   - Take turns massaging each other, focusing on relaxation and connection.

5. **Sensory Exploration**
   - Use the blindfold or silk scarf to heighten your partner's senses.
   - Introduce different textures and sensations, such as feathers, ice, or warm oil.

6. **Role-Playing and Fantasy**
   - Transition into a role-playing scenario or explore a new fantasy.
   - Ensure that both partners are comfortable and excited about the activities.

7. **Reflection and Journaling**
   - After your experience, take some time to reflect and journal about your feelings and intentions.
   - Share your thoughts with your partner and discuss any new insights or desires.

By embracing the energy of the New Moon, you can rejuvenate your sexual relationship and explore new depths of intimacy and connection. Use this time to set intentions, try new things, and create a fresh start in your sexual journey.

Chapter 15: Waxing Crescent - Building Anticipation
Influence of the Waxing Crescent on Sexual Energy and Kinks
The Waxing Crescent Moon follows the New Moon and marks a period of growth, momentum, and building energy. Astrologically, this phase is associated with the gradual increase of light and energy, making it an ideal time for planning, setting goals, and taking the first steps towards new endeavors. This phase enhances sexual energy by fostering a sense of anticipation, excitement, and curiosity about what lies ahead.

Key Influences of the Waxing Crescent on Sexual Energy

1. **Growing Excitement**
    - The Waxing Crescent phase is characterized by a growing sense of excitement and anticipation.
    - This period is perfect for building sexual tension and exploring new possibilities in the bedroom.

2. **Increased Motivation**
    - As the moon's light increases, so does motivation and drive.
    - This phase is ideal for setting and pursuing sexual goals, as well as exploring new kinks and practices.

3. **Playful Exploration**
    - The Waxing Crescent phase encourages playful exploration and experimentation.
    - Couples may feel more adventurous and willing to try new things during this time.

4. **Building Connection**
    - This phase is about building and strengthening connections.
    - It's an excellent time for deepening emotional and physical intimacy with your partner.

5. **Setting the Stage**
    - The Waxing Crescent is perfect for setting the stage for future experiences.

- It's a time to prepare, plan, and lay the groundwork for sexual activities and fantasies.

Common Sexual Kinks Associated with the Waxing Crescent

The Waxing Crescent's influence encourages anticipation and playful exploration. Here are some kinks that align well with the energy of this phase:

1. **Teasing and Edging**
   - Building anticipation through teasing and edging can be incredibly arousing.
   - Slowly bringing your partner to the edge of orgasm and then easing off can heighten sexual tension and pleasure.

2. **Sensory Play**
   - Engaging in sensory play can build anticipation and enhance the overall experience.
   - Introducing elements like feathers, ice, and different textures can create a heightened sense of arousal.

3. **Role-Playing**
   - The Waxing Crescent is a great time to explore new role-playing scenarios.
   - Trying out different characters and fantasies can add excitement and anticipation to your sexual encounters.

4. **Prolonged Foreplay**
   - Extending the foreplay phase can build sexual tension and anticipation.
   - Focus on exploring each other's bodies, kissing, and touching to create a slow build-up to intercourse.

5. **Erotic Communication**
   - Engaging in dirty talk, sexting, and sharing fantasies can build anticipation and excitement.
   - Communicating your desires and intentions can enhance the overall experience.

Recommended Kinks and Practices for Anticipation

To fully harness the energy of the Waxing Crescent, it's essential to focus on kinks and practices that build anticipation, excitement, and connection. Here are some recommendations:

1. **Teasing and Edging**
   - Practice teasing and edging techniques to build anticipation.
   - Use slow, deliberate touches and bring your partner close to orgasm multiple times before allowing them to climax.

2. **Sensory Exploration**
   - Engage in sensory play that introduces new and exciting sensations.
   - Use blindfolds, feathers, ice cubes, or warming oils to stimulate different senses and build anticipation.

3. **Prolonged Foreplay**
   - Extend the foreplay phase to build sexual tension.
   - Focus on kissing, touching, and exploring each other's bodies without rushing to intercourse.

4. **Role-Playing Scenarios**
   - Choose new and exciting role-playing scenarios to explore.
   - Encourage each other to step into different characters and fantasies that build anticipation.

5. **Erotic Communication**
   - Enhance anticipation through dirty talk, sexting, and sharing fantasies.
   - Communicate your desires and intentions to build excitement and connection.

6. **Planned Surprises**
   - Plan surprise sexual encounters or activities to build anticipation.
   - Create an element of mystery and excitement by leaving clues or hints for your partner.

Sample Waxing Crescent Ritual for Building Anticipation
Materials Needed:

- Candles (preferably white or green)
- Essential oils (such as peppermint, jasmine, or eucalyptus)
- A blindfold or silk scarf
- Feathers, ice cubes, or other sensory items
- Comfortable cushions or a soft blanket
- A journal and pen

Steps:

1. **Create a Sensory Space**
   - Set up a comfortable area with cushions, blankets, and your chosen materials.
   - Light the candles and use essential oils to create a stimulating and inviting atmosphere.
2. **Set Intentions Together**
   - Sit with your partner and take a few deep breaths together.
   - Share your sexual intentions and desires for the Waxing Crescent phase.
3. **Meditate and Connect**
   - Spend a few minutes meditating together, focusing on your breath and the connection between you.
   - Visualize building sexual energy and anticipation.
4. **Sensory Exploration**
   - Begin with sensory exploration using the blindfold or silk scarf.
   - Introduce different textures and sensations, such as feathers, ice, or warming oils, to build anticipation.
5. **Prolonged Foreplay**
   - Transition into prolonged foreplay, focusing on kissing, touching, and exploring each other's bodies.

- Take your time and build sexual tension without rushing to intercourse.

6. **Teasing and Edging**
   - Practice teasing and edging techniques to heighten anticipation.
   - Bring your partner close to orgasm multiple times before allowing them to climax.

7. **Role-Playing and Communication**
   - Incorporate a role-playing scenario or engage in dirty talk and sharing fantasies.
   - Communicate your desires and intentions to build excitement and connection.

8. **Reflection and Journaling**
   - After your experience, take some time to reflect and journal about your feelings and intentions.
   - Share your thoughts with your partner and discuss any new insights or desires.

By embracing the energy of the Waxing Crescent, you can build anticipation and excitement in your sexual relationship. Use this time to explore new kinks, deepen your connection, and set the stage for future sexual adventures.

Chapter 16: First Quarter - Taking Action
Influence of the First Quarter on Sexual Energy and Kinks

The First Quarter Moon marks a period of action, decision-making, and overcoming challenges. Astrologically, this phase is about taking the initial steps towards goals set during the New Moon and Waxing Crescent phases. The energy of the First Quarter Moon encourages movement, assertiveness, and progress, making it an ideal time for taking initiative and exploring new dynamics in sexual relationships.

Key Influences of the First Quarter on Sexual Energy

1. **Increased Motivation and Drive**
    ◦ The First Quarter phase brings a surge of energy and motivation.
    ◦ This period is perfect for acting on sexual desires and fantasies with confidence and enthusiasm.

2. **Decisiveness and Clarity**
    ◦ This phase is characterized by decisiveness and clarity.
    ◦ It's a great time to make decisions about sexual boundaries, desires, and new experiences.

3. **Assertiveness and Boldness**
    ◦ The First Quarter Moon enhances assertiveness and boldness.
    ◦ Couples may feel more confident in expressing their desires and taking control in the bedroom.

4. **Overcoming Challenges**
    ◦ This phase encourages overcoming obstacles and pushing past limitations.

- ○ It's an excellent time to address and resolve any sexual issues or inhibitions.

5. **Building Momentum**
   - ○ The energy of the First Quarter Moon is about building momentum and making progress.
   - ○ It's a perfect time to introduce new kinks and practices into your sexual routine.

Common Sexual Kinks Associated with the First Quarter

The First Quarter's influence encourages assertiveness, exploration, and taking action. Here are some kinks that align well with the energy of this phase:

1. **Dominance and Submission**
   - ○ The assertive energy of the First Quarter Moon is ideal for exploring dominance and submission dynamics.
   - ○ Taking control or surrendering can enhance sexual experiences and build trust.

2. **Role-Playing**
   - ○ This phase is perfect for acting out bold and decisive role-playing scenarios.
   - ○ Exploring characters that involve power dynamics, such as boss/employee or master/slave, can be thrilling.

3. **Impact Play**
   - ○ The increased motivation and drive make impact play, such as spanking, flogging, or paddling, particularly appealing.
   - ○ These activities can heighten sensations and create a sense of assertiveness.

4. **Edging and Orgasm Control**
   - ○ Taking control of your partner's pleasure through edging and orgasm control can be highly arousing.
   - ○ This practice builds anticipation and enhances the overall experience.

5. Adventurous Sex

- The bold energy of this phase is perfect for exploring adventurous sex, such as outdoor or semi-public encounters.
- Trying new locations or positions can add excitement and spontaneity.

Recommended Kinks and Practices for Initiative

To fully harness the energy of the First Quarter, it's essential to focus on kinks and practices that encourage assertiveness, action, and progress. Here are some recommendations:

1. Dominance and Submission Dynamics

- Engage in dominance and submission dynamics to explore power and control.
- Use commands, restraints, and clear communication to create an intense and thrilling experience.

2. Role-Playing Scenarios

- Choose bold and decisive role-playing scenarios to act out.
- Encourage each other to step into characters that involve assertiveness and control.

3. Impact Play

- Introduce impact play elements such as spanking, flogging, or paddling.
- Ensure that the experience is safe, consensual, and enhances sensations and arousal.

4. Edging and Orgasm Control

- Practice edging and orgasm control techniques to build anticipation and heighten pleasure.
- Take turns controlling each other's pleasure to create a dynamic and exciting experience.

5. Adventurous Sex

- Plan adventurous sexual encounters in new or unexpected locations.

- ° Explore different positions, settings, or activities that add excitement and spontaneity.

6. **Clear Communication and Decision-Making**
   - ° Use the decisiveness of this phase to communicate desires and boundaries clearly.
   - ° Make decisions about new experiences and practices together, ensuring mutual consent and enthusiasm.

Sample First Quarter Ritual for Taking Action
Materials Needed:

- Candles (preferably red or orange)
- Essential oils (such as cedarwood, ginger, or sandalwood)
- Restraints (such as handcuffs, silk scarves, or ropes)
- Impact play tools (such as a paddle, flogger, or spanking glove)
- Comfortable cushions or a soft blanket
- A journal and pen

Steps:

1. **Create a Dynamic Space**
   - ° Set up a comfortable area with cushions, blankets, and your chosen materials.
   - ° Light the candles and use essential oils to create an energizing and inviting atmosphere.
2. **Set Intentions Together**
   - ° Sit with your partner and take a few deep breaths together.
   - ° Share your sexual intentions and desires for the First Quarter phase.
3. **Meditate and Connect**
   - ° Spend a few minutes meditating together, focusing on your breath and the connection between you.

- ○ Visualize taking action and making progress in your sexual relationship.

4. **Dominance and Submission Dynamics**
   - ○ Begin exploring dominance and submission dynamics using commands, restraints, and clear communication.
   - ○ Take turns being in control or surrendering to enhance trust and intensity.

5. **Impact Play**
   - ○ Introduce impact play elements such as spanking, flogging, or paddling.
   - ○ Start slowly and build intensity, ensuring that the experience is safe and consensual.

6. **Role-Playing and Communication**
   - ○ Incorporate a bold and decisive role-playing scenario.
   - ○ Communicate your desires and intentions clearly to build excitement and connection.

7. **Edging and Orgasm Control**
   - ○ Practice edging and orgasm control techniques to heighten anticipation and pleasure.
   - ○ Take turns controlling each other's pleasure to create a dynamic and thrilling experience.

8. **Reflection and Journaling**
   - ○ After your experience, take some time to reflect and journal about your feelings and intentions.
   - ○ Share your thoughts with your partner and discuss any new insights or desires.

By embracing the energy of the First Quarter, you can take action and make significant progress in your sexual relationship. Use this time to explore new dynamics, enhance your connection, and build momentum for future sexual adventures.

Chapter 17: Waxing Gibbous - Refinement and Focus
Influence of the Waxing Gibbous on Sexual Energy and Kinks
The Waxing Gibbous Moon follows the First Quarter phase and leads up to the Full Moon. This period is characterized by refinement, focus, and preparation for culmination. Astrologically, it's a time to fine-tune efforts, pay attention to details, and ensure that plans are coming together smoothly. The energy of the Waxing Gibbous Moon encourages polishing and perfecting, making it an ideal time for refining sexual practices and focusing on deepening intimacy.

Key Influences of the Waxing Gibbous on Sexual Energy

1. **Refinement and Attention to Detail**
   - The Waxing Gibbous phase is about refining and perfecting.
   - This period is perfect for focusing on the finer details of sexual experiences, enhancing techniques, and improving intimacy.

2. **Increased Focus and Dedication**
   - This phase brings heightened focus and dedication.
   - It's a great time to invest in improving sexual skills and deepening the connection with your partner.

3. **Building Anticipation**
   - As the moon grows towards fullness, there is a natural build-up of anticipation.
   - This phase is ideal for slowly building sexual tension and anticipation, leading to a more satisfying climax.

4. **Nurturing and Enhancing**
   - The Waxing Gibbous phase encourages nurturing and enhancing what has already been started.
   - It's an excellent time to nurture the emotional and physical aspects of your sexual relationship.

5. **Preparation for Fulfillment**
   - This period is about preparing for the culmination of efforts.
   - It's a perfect time to ensure that you and your partner are aligned and ready for deeply fulfilling sexual experiences.

Common Sexual Kinks Associated with the Waxing Gibbous

The Waxing Gibbous's influence encourages refinement, focus, and building anticipation. Here are some kinks that align well with the energy of this phase:

1. **Edging and Orgasm Control**
   - Refining the practice of edging and orgasm control can heighten pleasure and anticipation.
   - Slowly building up to orgasm multiple times can enhance the overall sexual experience.
2. **Sensory Play**
   - Enhancing sensory play with a focus on refinement can create deeply stimulating experiences.
   - Using a variety of textures, temperatures, and sensations can refine the sensory experience.
3. **Erotic Massage**
   - Focusing on the details of an erotic massage can deepen intimacy and connection.
   - Using specific techniques and paying attention to your partner's responses can enhance the experience.
4. **Tantric Practices**
   - Refining tantric practices can enhance emotional and physical intimacy.
   - Focusing on breathing techniques, eye contact, and slow, deliberate movements can create a profound connection.

5. **Bondage and Discipline**
    ◦ Refining bondage and discipline practices can enhance control and trust.
    ◦ Using precise techniques and clear communication can create a safe and thrilling experience.

Recommended Kinks and Practices for Refinement

To fully harness the energy of the Waxing Gibbous, it's essential to focus on kinks and practices that encourage refinement, focus, and deepening intimacy. Here are some recommendations:

1. **Edging and Orgasm Control**
    ◦ Practice refining edging and orgasm control techniques.
    ◦ Use slow, deliberate touches and bring your partner close to orgasm multiple times before allowing them to climax.

2. **Sensory Exploration**
    ◦ Enhance sensory play with a focus on refinement.
    ◦ Introduce new textures, temperatures, and sensations to create a heightened sensory experience.

3. **Erotic Massage**
    ◦ Focus on the details of an erotic massage to deepen intimacy.
    ◦ Use specific techniques and pay attention to your partner's responses to enhance the experience.

4. **Tantric Practices**
    ◦ Refine tantric sex practices to enhance emotional and physical intimacy.
    ◦ Focus on breathing techniques, eye contact, and slow, deliberate movements to create a profound connection.

5. **Bondage and Discipline**
    ◦ Refine bondage and discipline practices to enhance control and trust.

○ Use precise techniques and clear communication to create a safe and thrilling experience.

6. **Clear Communication and Feedback**
   ○ Use the increased focus of this phase to communicate desires and feedback clearly.
   ○ Ensure mutual consent and enthusiasm for all activities to enhance the overall experience.

Sample Waxing Gibbous Ritual for Refinement and Focus Materials Needed:

- Candles (preferably blue or violet)
- Essential oils (such as lavender, chamomile, or sandalwood)
- Restraints (such as handcuffs, silk scarves, or ropes)
- Sensory play items (such as feathers, ice cubes, or warming oils)
- Comfortable cushions or a soft blanket
- A journal and pen

Steps:

1. **Create a Focused Space**
   ○ Set up a comfortable area with cushions, blankets, and your chosen materials.
   ○ Light the candles and use essential oils to create a calming and focused atmosphere.
2. **Set Intentions Together**
   ○ Sit with your partner and take a few deep breaths together.
   ○ Share your sexual intentions and desires for the Waxing Gibbous phase.
3. **Meditate and Connect**
   ○ Spend a few minutes meditating together, focusing on your breath and the connection between you.
   ○ Visualize refining and enhancing your sexual relationship.

4. **Edging and Orgasm Control**
   - Practice refining edging and orgasm control techniques.
   - Use slow, deliberate touches and bring your partner close to orgasm multiple times before allowing them to climax.

5. **Sensory Exploration**
   - Enhance sensory play with a focus on refinement.
   - Introduce new textures, temperatures, and sensations to create a heightened sensory experience.

6. **Erotic Massage**
   - Focus on the details of an erotic massage to deepen intimacy.
   - Use specific techniques and pay attention to your partner's responses to enhance the experience.

7. **Tantric Practices and Bondage**
   - Refine tantric practices and introduce precise bondage techniques.
   - Focus on breathing techniques, eye contact, and clear communication to create a safe and thrilling experience.

8. **Reflection and Journaling**
   - After your experience, take some time to reflect and journal about your feelings and intentions.
   - Share your thoughts with your partner and discuss any new insights or desires.

By embracing the energy of the Waxing Gibbous, you can refine and enhance your sexual relationship. Use this time to focus on the finer details, deepen your connection, and prepare for deeply fulfilling sexual experiences.

Chapter 18: Full Moon - Peak Passion
Influence of the Full Moon on Sexual Energy and Kinks

The Full Moon represents the pinnacle of the lunar cycle, a time when the moon is fully illuminated and its energy is at its peak. Astrologically, the Full Moon is associated with heightened emotions, increased energy, and the culmination of efforts. This phase brings a sense of completion, celebration, and intense passion. The energy of the Full Moon amplifies sexual desires, making it an ideal time for exploring intense and passionate experiences.

Key Influences of the Full Moon on Sexual Energy

1. **Heightened Emotions and Sensitivity**
   - The Full Moon enhances emotional sensitivity and depth.
   - This period is perfect for exploring deep emotional connections and intense feelings during sexual encounters.

2. **Increased Libido and Passion**
   - The energy of the Full Moon boosts libido and passion.
   - Couples may feel a strong desire to connect physically and emotionally, leading to more intense sexual experiences.

3. **Culmination and Celebration**
   - The Full Moon marks the culmination of efforts and intentions set earlier in the lunar cycle.
   - It's a time to celebrate achievements and enjoy the fruits of your labor, both in and out of the bedroom.

4. **Release and Letting Go**
   - This phase encourages the release of pent-up energy and emotions.
   - It's an excellent time to explore activities that involve intense physical and emotional release.

5. **Heightened Sensory Awareness**
   - The Full Moon enhances sensory awareness, making touch, taste, and other sensations more intense.

- This is a perfect time to indulge in sensory-rich experiences and kinks.

Common Sexual Kinks Associated with the Full Moon

The Full Moon's influence encourages passion, intensity, and deep emotional connections. Here are some kinks that align well with the energy of this phase:

1. **Intense Bondage and Discipline**
   - The heightened emotions and passion of the Full Moon are ideal for exploring intense bondage and discipline dynamics.
   - Using restraints, blindfolds, and impact play can create a powerful and thrilling experience.
2. **Tantric Practices**
   - The Full Moon's energy aligns well with tantric practices that focus on prolonged intimacy and deep connection.
   - These practices can enhance the emotional and spiritual bond between partners.
3. **Role-Playing and Fantasy Exploration**
   - This phase is perfect for acting out bold and intense role-playing scenarios.
   - Exploring characters and fantasies that involve deep emotional connections and intensity can be highly arousing.
4. **Sensory Overload**
   - The heightened sensory awareness of the Full Moon is ideal for sensory overload play.
   - Using multiple sensory stimuli simultaneously can create an overwhelming and exhilarating experience.
5. **Rough and Passionate Sex**
   - The increased libido and passion make rough and passionate sex particularly appealing.

○ Engaging in intense, vigorous, and spontaneous sex can be deeply satisfying.

Recommended Kinks and Practices for Passion

To fully harness the energy of the Full Moon, it's essential to focus on kinks and practices that encourage intense passion, deep connection, and emotional release. Here are some recommendations:

1. **Intense Bondage and Discipline**
   - ○ Explore intense bondage and discipline dynamics to enhance control and trust.
   - ○ Use restraints, blindfolds, and impact play to create a powerful and thrilling experience.

2. **Tantric Practices**
   - ○ Engage in tantric sex practices to deepen emotional and physical intimacy.
   - ○ Focus on breathing techniques, eye contact, and prolonged touch to create a profound connection.

3. **Role-Playing and Fantasy Exploration**
   - ○ Choose bold and intense role-playing scenarios to act out.
   - ○ Encourage each other to step into characters and fantasies that involve deep emotional connections and intensity.

4. **Sensory Overload**
   - ○ Introduce sensory overload play to heighten sensory awareness.
   - ○ Use multiple sensory stimuli, such as feathers, ice, scented oils, and music, to create an overwhelming experience.

5. **Rough and Passionate Sex**
   - ○ Embrace the heightened libido and passion of the Full Moon by engaging in rough and passionate sex.

- Focus on intense, vigorous, and spontaneous encounters to satisfy your desires.

6. **Emotional Release and Connection**
   - Use the Full Moon's energy to explore activities that involve emotional release and deep connection.
   - Engage in activities that allow for the expression of emotions and the deepening of your bond.

Sample Full Moon Ritual for Peak Passion
Materials Needed:

- Candles (preferably red or gold)
- Essential oils (such as ylang-ylang, patchouli, or sandalwood)
- Restraints (such as handcuffs, silk scarves, or ropes)
- Sensory play items (such as feathers, ice cubes, scented oils)
- Comfortable cushions or a soft blanket
- A journal and pen

Steps:

1. **Create an Intense Space**
   - Set up a comfortable area with cushions, blankets, and your chosen materials.
   - Light the candles and use essential oils to create a passionate and inviting atmosphere.
2. **Set Intentions Together**
   - Sit with your partner and take a few deep breaths together.
   - Share your sexual intentions and desires for the Full Moon phase.
3. **Meditate and Connect**
   - Spend a few minutes meditating together, focusing on your breath and the connection between you.

- ◦ Visualize experiencing intense passion and deep connection during your sexual encounters.

4. **Intense Bondage and Discipline**
   - ◦ Begin exploring intense bondage and discipline dynamics using restraints, blindfolds, and impact play.
   - ◦ Take turns being in control or surrendering to enhance trust and intensity.

5. **Tantric Practices**
   - ◦ Engage in tantric practices to deepen emotional and physical intimacy.
   - ◦ Focus on breathing techniques, eye contact, and prolonged touch to create a profound connection.

6. **Role-Playing and Sensory Overload**
   - ◦ Incorporate a bold and intense role-playing scenario.
   - ◦ Introduce sensory overload play using multiple sensory stimuli, such as feathers, ice, scented oils, and music.

7. **Rough and Passionate Sex**
   - ◦ Embrace the heightened libido and passion of the Full Moon by engaging in rough and passionate sex.
   - ◦ Focus on intense, vigorous, and spontaneous encounters to satisfy your desires.

8. **Emotional Release and Connection**
   - ◦ Use the Full Moon's energy to explore activities that involve emotional release and deep connection.
   - ◦ Allow for the expression of emotions and the deepening of your bond.

9. **Reflection and Journaling**
   - ◦ After your experience, take some time to reflect and journal about your feelings and intentions.
   - ◦ Share your thoughts with your partner and discuss any new insights or desires.

By embracing the energy of the Full Moon, you can experience peak passion and deepen your sexual relationship. Use this time to explore intense kinks, enhance your connection, and celebrate the culmination of your efforts.

Chapter 19: Waning Gibbous - Gratitude and Sharing
Influence of the Waning Gibbous on Sexual Energy and Kinks
The Waning Gibbous Moon follows the Full Moon and marks the beginning of the moon's decrease in illumination. This phase is characterized by a time of reflection, gratitude, and sharing the results of what has been accomplished during the waxing phases and Full Moon. Astrologically, it is a time to give thanks, appreciate, and disseminate knowledge and experiences. The energy of the Waning Gibbous Moon encourages openness, connection, and the sharing of intimacy and gratitude, making it an ideal time for deepening bonds and exploring mutual pleasure.

Key Influences of the Waning Gibbous on Sexual Energy

1. **Gratitude and Reflection**
   - The Waning Gibbous phase encourages reflection on recent experiences and a sense of gratitude.
   - This period is perfect for appreciating the sexual connection and growth achieved with your partner.

2. **Sharing and Generosity**
   - This phase fosters a sense of generosity and sharing.
   - It's an excellent time for giving and receiving pleasure, focusing on mutual satisfaction.

3. **Connection and Openness**
   - The energy of the Waning Gibbous Moon enhances emotional connection and openness.
   - Couples may feel more inclined to communicate and share their deepest feelings and desires.

4. **Mutual Exploration**
   - This phase is about exploring mutual pleasure and discovering new aspects of each other.

- ◦ It's a great time for experimenting with new kinks and practices together.

5. **Nurturing and Support**
   - ◦ The Waning Gibbous Moon promotes nurturing and supportive behaviors.
   - ◦ It's an ideal time to care for each other's needs and build a stronger emotional and physical bond.

Common Sexual Kinks Associated with the Waning Gibbous

The Waning Gibbous's influence encourages sharing, generosity, and mutual exploration. Here are some kinks that align well with the energy of this phase:

1. **Mutual Masturbation**
   - ◦ Sharing the experience of mutual masturbation can enhance intimacy and openness.
   - ◦ This practice allows partners to explore each other's bodies and desires together.

2. **Sensual Massage**
   - ◦ Giving and receiving sensual massages can create a deep sense of connection and relaxation.
   - ◦ Focus on nurturing touch and mutual pleasure to strengthen the bond.

3. **Sharing Fantasies**
   - ◦ The Waning Gibbous phase is perfect for sharing and exploring fantasies.
   - ◦ Open communication about desires can lead to a deeper understanding and connection.

4. **Oral Sex**
   - ◦ Engaging in oral sex with a focus on mutual pleasure and satisfaction can be deeply intimate.
   - ◦ Taking turns giving and receiving can enhance the sense of sharing and generosity.

5. **Exploring New Kinks Together**
    - This phase encourages mutual exploration of new kinks and practices.
    - Experimenting with new activities together can be exciting and build trust.

Recommended Kinks and Practices for Sharing

To fully harness the energy of the Waning Gibbous, it's essential to focus on kinks and practices that encourage sharing, generosity, and deepening connection. Here are some recommendations:

1. **Mutual Masturbation**
    - Practice mutual masturbation to explore each other's bodies and desires together.
    - Take turns guiding each other to enhance intimacy and openness.
2. **Sensual Massage**
    - Give and receive sensual massages to create a deep sense of connection and relaxation.
    - Use scented oils and focus on nurturing touch to enhance the experience.
3. **Sharing Fantasies**
    - Openly communicate and share fantasies with your partner.
    - Discuss desires and explore ways to incorporate them into your sexual experiences.
4. **Oral Sex**
    - Focus on mutual pleasure and satisfaction through oral sex.
    - Take turns giving and receiving to enhance the sense of sharing and generosity.
5. **Exploring New Kinks Together**
    - Experiment with new kinks and practices together.

- Choose activities that both partners are curious about and excited to try.

6. **Clear Communication and Feedback**
   - Use the openness of this phase to communicate desires and feedback clearly.
   - Ensure mutual consent and enthusiasm for all activities to enhance the overall experience.

Sample Waning Gibbous Ritual for Gratitude and Sharing Materials Needed:

- Candles (preferably white or yellow)
- Essential oils (such as rose, vanilla, or lavender)
- Sensual massage oils
- Comfortable cushions or a soft blanket
- A journal and pen

Steps:

1. **Create a Nurturing Space**
   - Set up a comfortable area with cushions, blankets, and your chosen materials.
   - Light the candles and use essential oils to create a calming and nurturing atmosphere.
2. **Set Intentions Together**
   - Sit with your partner and take a few deep breaths together.
   - Share your sexual intentions and desires for the Waning Gibbous phase.
3. **Meditate and Connect**
   - Spend a few minutes meditating together, focusing on your breath and the connection between you.
   - Visualize experiencing deep connection, gratitude, and mutual pleasure during your sexual encounters.

4. **Mutual Masturbation**
   - Begin with mutual masturbation to explore each other's bodies and desires.
   - Take turns guiding each other and sharing what feels good.

5. **Sensual Massage**
   - Give and receive sensual massages to create a deep sense of connection and relaxation.
   - Use scented oils and focus on nurturing touch to enhance the experience.

6. **Sharing Fantasies**
   - Openly communicate and share fantasies with your partner.
   - Discuss desires and explore ways to incorporate them into your sexual experiences.

7. **Oral Sex and New Kinks**
   - Focus on mutual pleasure and satisfaction through oral sex.
   - Experiment with new kinks and practices that both partners are curious about and excited to try.

8. **Reflection and Journaling**
   - After your experience, take some time to reflect and journal about your feelings and intentions.
   - Share your thoughts with your partner and discuss any new insights or desires.

By embracing the energy of the Waning Gibbous, you can deepen your sexual relationship through gratitude, sharing, and mutual exploration. Use this time to enhance your connection, explore new kinks, and appreciate the growth and intimacy you've achieved together.

Chapter 20: Last Quarter - Reflection and Release
Influence of the Last Quarter on Sexual Energy and Kinks
The Last Quarter Moon follows the Waning Gibbous phase and leads up to the New Moon. This period is characterized by reflection, assessment, and letting go. Astrologically, it's a time to evaluate what has been accomplished, understand lessons learned, and release what no longer serves us. The energy of the Last Quarter Moon encourages introspection, understanding, and purification, making it an ideal time for reflecting on sexual experiences and letting go of inhibitions or past negative experiences.

Key Influences of the Last Quarter on Sexual Energy

1. **Reflection and Introspection**
   - The Last Quarter phase encourages deep reflection and introspection.
   - This period is perfect for evaluating your sexual relationship, understanding what has worked, and identifying areas for improvement.

2. **Releasing Negativity and Inhibitions**
   - This phase is about letting go of negative emotions, past traumas, and inhibitions.
   - It's an excellent time to release anything that hinders your sexual growth and intimacy.

3. **Purification and Healing**
   - The Last Quarter Moon promotes purification and healing.
   - This is an ideal time to engage in practices that cleanse and rejuvenate your sexual energy.

4. **Assessment and Adjustment**
   - This phase encourages assessment and adjustment of sexual practices and dynamics.

  - It's a great time to discuss and make necessary changes to enhance mutual satisfaction.

5. **Emotional Release and Connection**
   - The energy of the Last Quarter Moon supports emotional release and deep connection.
   - Couples may feel more inclined to share their feelings, vulnerabilities, and desires.

Common Sexual Kinks Associated with the Last Quarter

The Last Quarter's influence encourages reflection, release, and healing. Here are some kinks that align well with the energy of this phase:

1. **Emotional Bondage**
   - Emotional bondage involves using psychological and emotional elements to enhance intimacy.
   - This practice can help release emotional barriers and deepen the connection between partners.

2. **Tantric Practices**
   - Tantric sex practices that focus on healing and purification align well with the Last Quarter Moon.
   - These practices can facilitate emotional release and spiritual connection.

3. **Sensory Deprivation**
   - Sensory deprivation, such as using blindfolds or earplugs, can enhance introspection and focus.
   - This practice can help partners tune into their inner experiences and connect on a deeper level.

4. **Impact Play for Release**
   - Impact play, when done consensually and safely, can facilitate the release of pent-up emotions.

- Activities like spanking or flogging can provide a cathartic experience.

5. **Cleansing Rituals**
   - Engaging in cleansing rituals, such as baths or showers together, can symbolize purification and renewal.
   - This practice can help release negativity and foster a fresh start.

Recommended Kinks and Practices for Reflection

To fully harness the energy of the Last Quarter, it's essential to focus on kinks and practices that encourage reflection, release, and healing. Here are some recommendations:

1. **Emotional Bondage**
   - Engage in emotional bondage to explore psychological and emotional intimacy.
   - Use affirmations, eye contact, and verbal communication to deepen the connection.

2. **Tantric Practices**
   - Practice tantric sex to facilitate healing and purification.
   - Focus on breathing techniques, eye contact, and slow, deliberate movements to create a profound connection.

3. **Sensory Deprivation**
   - Use sensory deprivation to enhance introspection and focus.
   - Blindfolds, earplugs, or other sensory deprivation tools can help partners tune into their inner experiences.

4. **Impact Play for Release**
   - Engage in impact play to facilitate the release of pent-up emotions.

    ◦ Ensure that the experience is consensual, safe, and provides a cathartic release.

5. **Cleansing Rituals**
   - Perform cleansing rituals, such as taking baths or showers together.
   - Use this time to symbolize purification and renewal, releasing negativity and fostering a fresh start.

6. **Clear Communication and Feedback**
   - Use the reflective energy of this phase to communicate desires and feedback clearly.
   - Ensure mutual consent and understanding for all activities to enhance the overall experience.

Sample Last Quarter Ritual for Reflection and Release
Materials Needed:

- Candles (preferably blue or white)
- Essential oils (such as eucalyptus, tea tree, or lavender)
- Blindfolds or earplugs for sensory deprivation
- Impact play tools (such as a paddle, flogger, or spanking glove)
- Bath or shower supplies for cleansing rituals
- Comfortable cushions or a soft blanket
- A journal and pen

Steps:

1. **Create a Reflective Space**
   - Set up a comfortable area with cushions, blankets, and your chosen materials.
   - Light the candles and use essential oils to create a calming and reflective atmosphere.

2. **Set Intentions Together**
   - Sit with your partner and take a few deep breaths together.
   - Share your sexual intentions and desires for the Last Quarter phase.

3. **Meditate and Connect**
   - Spend a few minutes meditating together, focusing on your breath and the connection between you.
   - Visualize experiencing reflection, release, and healing during your sexual encounters.

4. **Emotional Bondage**
   - Engage in emotional bondage to explore psychological and emotional intimacy.
   - Use affirmations, eye contact, and verbal communication to deepen the connection.

5. **Tantric Practices**
   - Practice tantric sex to facilitate healing and purification.
   - Focus on breathing techniques, eye contact, and slow, deliberate movements to create a profound connection.

6. **Sensory Deprivation**
   - Use sensory deprivation tools, such as blindfolds or earplugs, to enhance introspection and focus.
   - Tune into your inner experiences and connect on a deeper level.

7. **Impact Play for Release**
   - Engage in impact play to facilitate the release of pent-up emotions.
   - Ensure that the experience is consensual, safe, and provides a cathartic release.

8. **Cleansing Rituals**
   - Perform cleansing rituals, such as taking baths or showers together.
   - Use this time to symbolize purification and renewal, releasing negativity and fostering a fresh start.

9. **Reflection and Journaling**
    ◦ After your experience, take some time to reflect and journal about your feelings and intentions.
    ◦ Share your thoughts with your partner and discuss any new insights or desires.

By embracing the energy of the Last Quarter, you can deepen your sexual relationship through reflection, release, and healing. Use this time to evaluate your experiences, release inhibitions, and foster a fresh start for your sexual journey.

Chapter 21: Waning Crescent - Rest and Preparation
Influence of the Waning Crescent on Sexual Energy and Kinks
The Waning Crescent Moon is the final phase of the lunar cycle before the New Moon. This period is characterized by rest, recuperation, and preparation for new beginnings. Astrologically, it is a time to retreat, reflect, and recharge. The energy of the Waning Crescent Moon encourages relaxation, introspection, and setting the stage for future growth. This phase is ideal for resting, healing, and preparing for the upcoming cycle, making it an excellent time for gentle, nurturing sexual practices that focus on comfort and connection.

Key Influences of the Waning Crescent on Sexual Energy

1. **Rest and Recuperation**
   - The Waning Crescent phase is about rest and recuperation.
   - This period is perfect for taking a break from intense activities and focusing on relaxation and healing.

2. **Introspection and Reflection**
   - This phase encourages introspection and reflection on recent experiences.
   - It's a great time to consider what has been learned and prepare for future growth.

3. **Nurturing and Comfort**
   - The energy of the Waning Crescent Moon fosters nurturing and comfort.

- ° It's an excellent time for gentle, comforting sexual practices that enhance emotional and physical well-being.

4. **Preparation for New Beginnings**
   - ° This phase is about preparing for new beginnings.
   - ° It's a perfect time to set intentions and plan for the upcoming lunar cycle.

5. **Emotional and Physical Healing**
   - ° The Waning Crescent Moon promotes emotional and physical healing.
   - ° This period is ideal for engaging in practices that support recovery and rejuvenation.

Common Sexual Kinks Associated with the Waning Crescent

The Waning Crescent's influence encourages rest, nurturing, and preparation. Here are some kinks that align well with the energy of this phase:

1. **Sensual Massage**
   - ° Sensual massage is perfect for rest and recuperation.
   - ° Using gentle touch and soothing oils can promote relaxation and healing.

2. **Cuddling and Holding**
   - ° This phase is ideal for cuddling and holding your partner.
   - ° Physical closeness without the need for intense activity can enhance emotional connection and comfort.

3. **Tantric Practices**
   - ° Gentle tantric practices that focus on relaxation and connection align well with the Waning Crescent Moon.
   - ° These practices can facilitate emotional and physical healing.

4. **Mindfulness and Meditation**
   - ° Engaging in mindfulness and meditation together can promote introspection and connection.

- These practices can help partners tune into their inner experiences and prepare for new beginnings.

5. **Gentle Bondage**
   - Gentle bondage practices, such as using soft scarves or silk ties, can enhance trust and comfort.
   - The focus should be on relaxation and gentle connection rather than intense sensations.

Recommended Kinks and Practices for Rest and Preparation

To fully harness the energy of the Waning Crescent, it's essential to focus on kinks and practices that encourage rest, nurturing, and preparation. Here are some recommendations:

1. **Sensual Massage**
   - Give and receive sensual massages to promote relaxation and healing.
   - Use gentle touch and soothing oils to enhance the experience.

2. **Cuddling and Holding**
   - Focus on cuddling and holding your partner to enhance emotional connection and comfort.
   - Physical closeness can promote a sense of security and well-being.

3. **Gentle Tantric Practices**
   - Practice gentle tantric sex to facilitate relaxation and connection.
   - Focus on breathing techniques, eye contact, and slow, deliberate movements to create a calming experience.

4. **Mindfulness and Meditation**
   - Engage in mindfulness and meditation together to promote introspection and connection.
   - Use these practices to tune into your inner experiences and prepare for new beginnings.

5. **Gentle Bondage**
    - Incorporate gentle bondage practices, such as using soft scarves or silk ties, to enhance trust and comfort.
    - Ensure that the focus is on relaxation and gentle connection rather than intense sensations.
6. **Clear Communication and Reflection**
    - Use the introspective energy of this phase to communicate desires and feedback clearly.
    - Reflect on recent experiences and discuss any new insights or intentions for the future.

Sample Waning Crescent Ritual for Rest and Preparation
Materials Needed:

- Candles (preferably blue or lavender)
- Essential oils (such as chamomile, lavender, or sandalwood)
- Sensual massage oils
- Soft scarves or silk ties for gentle bondage
- Comfortable cushions or a soft blanket
- A journal and pen

Steps:

1. **Create a Restful Space**
   - Set up a comfortable area with cushions, blankets, and your chosen materials.
   - Light the candles and use essential oils to create a calming and restful atmosphere.

2. **Set Intentions Together**
   - Sit with your partner and take a few deep breaths together.
   - Share your sexual intentions and desires for the Waning Crescent phase.

3. **Meditate and Connect**
   - Spend a few minutes meditating together, focusing on your breath and the connection between you.
   - Visualize experiencing rest, healing, and preparation for new beginnings during your sexual encounters.

4. **Sensual Massage**
   - Give and receive sensual massages to promote relaxation and healing.
   - Use gentle touch and soothing oils to enhance the experience.

5. **Cuddling and Holding**
   - Focus on cuddling and holding your partner to enhance emotional connection and comfort.
   - Physical closeness can promote a sense of security and well-being.

6. **Gentle Tantric Practices**
   - Practice gentle tantric sex to facilitate relaxation and connection.

- Focus on breathing techniques, eye contact, and slow, deliberate movements to create a calming experience.

7. **Mindfulness and Meditation**
- Engage in mindfulness and meditation together to promote introspection and connection.
- Use these practices to tune into your inner experiences and prepare for new beginnings.

8. **Gentle Bondage**
- Incorporate gentle bondage practices, such as using soft scarves or silk ties, to enhance trust and comfort.
- Ensure that the focus is on relaxation and gentle connection rather than intense sensations.

9. **Reflection and Journaling**
- After your experience, take some time to reflect and journal about your feelings and intentions.
- Share your thoughts with your partner and discuss any new insights or desires.

By embracing the energy of the Waning Crescent, you can focus on rest, nurturing, and preparation for new beginnings. Use this time to enhance your connection, promote healing, and set the stage for future growth in your sexual relationship.

Chapter 22: Cosmic Events and Their Influence on Sexuality Explanation of Various Cosmic Events and Their Astrological Significance

Cosmic events, such as eclipses, retrogrades, and meteor showers, have significant astrological implications and can greatly influence human behavior, emotions, and energy. These celestial occurrences often bring shifts in our lives, prompting changes, reflection, and new beginnings. Understanding these events and their astrological significance can help you harness their energy to enhance your sexual experiences and relationships.

Eclipses

Solar Eclipses:

- **Astrological Significance:** Solar eclipses occur when the moon passes between the Earth and the Sun, temporarily blocking the Sun's light. Astrologically, solar eclipses signify powerful new beginnings, sudden changes, and revelations. They are a time for setting new intentions and embarking on new paths.
- **Influence on Sexuality:** Solar eclipses can bring a surge of energy, motivation, and desire for transformation. This is a perfect time for exploring new sexual dynamics, trying new kinks, and setting fresh sexual intentions with your partner.

Lunar Eclipses:

- **Astrological Significance:** Lunar eclipses occur when the Earth comes between the Sun and the Moon, casting a shadow on the Moon. Astrologically, lunar eclipses represent culmination, closure, and the release of old patterns. They are a time for emotional revelations and letting go of what no longer serves you.

- **Influence on Sexuality:** Lunar eclipses can heighten emotions, increase sensitivity, and bring hidden desires to the surface. This is an ideal time for deep emotional connections, exploring fantasies, and releasing sexual inhibitions.

Retrogrades
Mercury Retrograde:

- **Astrological Significance:** Mercury retrograde occurs when the planet Mercury appears to move backward in its orbit. Astrologically, this period is associated with communication breakdowns, misunderstandings, and delays. It is a time for reflection, reassessment, and revisiting past issues.
- **Influence on Sexuality:** Mercury retrograde can cause misunderstandings and miscommunications in relationships. Use this time to revisit and resolve past sexual issues, improve communication with your partner, and explore slower, more thoughtful sexual practices.

Venus Retrograde:

- **Astrological Significance:** Venus retrograde occurs when Venus appears to move backward in its orbit. Astrologically, this period affects love, relationships, and self-worth. It is a time for reassessing relationships, revisiting past loves, and understanding your desires and values.
- **Influence on Sexuality:** Venus retrograde can bring past relationships and unresolved emotions to the forefront. This is a perfect time for exploring old fantasies, reconnecting with past partners, and reflecting on your sexual values and desires.

Mars Retrograde:

- **Astrological Significance:** Mars retrograde occurs when Mars appears to move backward in its orbit. Astrologically, this period affects energy, drive, and sexual desire. It is a time for reevaluating your goals, reassessing your actions, and managing frustrations.
- **Influence on Sexuality:** Mars retrograde can decrease sexual drive and increase frustration. Use this time to explore gentle, nurturing sexual practices, reflect on your sexual desires, and manage any pent-up energy through slow and mindful activities.

Meteor Showers
Perseid Meteor Shower:

- **Astrological Significance:** The Perseid meteor shower occurs annually in August, bringing a spectacular display of meteors. Astrologically, meteor showers signify inspiration, heightened intuition, and the manifestation of desires.
- **Influence on Sexuality:** The Perseid meteor shower can bring a sense of magic and inspiration to your sexual experiences. Use this time to explore romantic fantasies, engage in outdoor sexual activities under the stars, and manifest your deepest sexual desires.

Leonid Meteor Shower:

- **Astrological Significance:** The Leonid meteor shower occurs annually in November, bringing a dramatic display of meteors. Astrologically, meteor showers signify renewal, transformation, and the breaking of old patterns.
- **Influence on Sexuality:** The Leonid meteor shower can inspire transformation and renewal in your sexual relationship. Use this time to break free from old sexual routines, explore new kinks, and transform your sexual connection with your partner.

Recommended Kinks and Practices for Each Cosmic Event
Solar Eclipses
Recommended Kinks:

1. **Role-Playing:** Explore new roles and scenarios that symbolize new beginnings and transformations.
2. **Impact Play:** Use the surge of energy to engage in impact play, such as spanking or flogging, to heighten sensations and release pent-up energy.

Practices:

1. **Setting Intentions:** Use the energy of the solar eclipse to set new sexual intentions and goals with your partner.
2. **Exploring New Kinks:** Try new kinks and activities that you haven't explored before, embracing the theme of new beginnings.

Lunar Eclipses
Recommended Kinks:

1. **Sensory Deprivation:** Heighten emotional and physical sensitivity by using blindfolds or earplugs.
2. **Bondage:** Explore bondage to create a sense of vulnerability and emotional release.

Practices:

1. **Emotional Connection:** Focus on deep emotional connections through intimate conversations and eye contact during sex.
2. **Releasing Inhibitions:** Use the lunar eclipse to release sexual inhibitions and explore hidden desires.

Mercury Retrograde
Recommended Kinks:

1. **Erotic Writing:** Write and share erotic stories or fantasies with your partner to enhance communication.
2. **Mindfulness Practices:** Engage in slow, mindful sexual activities that promote relaxation and connection.

Practices:

1. **Improving Communication:** Focus on improving communication with your partner, discussing sexual desires, boundaries, and past issues.
2. **Reflecting on Past Experiences:** Revisit and reflect on past sexual experiences to gain insights and improve future encounters.

Venus Retrograde
Recommended Kinks:

1. **Sensual Massage:** Use sensual massage to reconnect with your partner and enhance intimacy.
2. **Reenacting Old Fantasies:** Revisit and reenact past fantasies to explore unresolved desires.

Practices:

1. **Reassessing Relationships:** Use this time to reassess your sexual relationship, discuss values, and understand each other's desires.
2. **Self-Love Practices:** Focus on self-love and self-care, exploring solo sexual activities to understand your own desires.

Mars Retrograde
Recommended Kinks:

1. **Tantric Practices:** Engage in tantric sex to promote slow, mindful connections and manage sexual energy.
2. **Gentle Bondage:** Use soft restraints to create a sense of security and comfort.

Practices:

1. **Managing Frustration:** Use slow, nurturing sexual practices to manage any frustration and decrease in sexual drive.
2. **Reflecting on Desires:** Reflect on your sexual desires and goals, and discuss them with your partner to align your energies.

Perseid Meteor Shower
Recommended Kinks:

1. **Outdoor Sex:** Embrace the magic of the meteor shower by engaging in outdoor sexual activities under the stars.
2. **Romantic Role-Playing:** Explore romantic fantasies and role-playing scenarios inspired by celestial themes.

Practices:

1. **Manifesting Desires:** Use the energy of the meteor shower to manifest your deepest sexual desires and intentions.
2. **Celebrating Love:** Celebrate your sexual connection with romantic gestures, such as stargazing or a candlelit dinner.

**Leonid Meteor Shower
Recommended Kinks:**

1. **Transformative Role-Playing:** Explore role-playing scenarios that symbolize transformation and renewal.
2. **Kink Exploration:** Break free from old routines by trying new kinks and activities that excite you.

Practices:

1. **Transforming Routines:** Use the energy of the meteor shower to transform your sexual routines and habits.
2. **Reconnecting with Passion:** Reignite passion in your relationship by exploring new sexual dynamics and practices.

By understanding the astrological significance of cosmic events and their influence on sexuality, you can enhance your sexual experiences and relationships. Use the energy of these events to explore new kinks, deepen connections, and set intentions for growth and transformation in your sexual journey.

Chapter 23: Planet Alignments and Sexual Compatibility
Explanation of Major Planet Alignments and Their Impact on Relationships and Sexuality

Planetary alignments, where multiple planets align or aspect each other in the sky, can have profound effects on human behavior, emotions, and relationships. Astrologically, these alignments create powerful energy shifts that influence our interactions, desires, and compatibility with others. Understanding the impact of these alignments can help you navigate your sexual and romantic relationships more effectively, using this cosmic energy to enhance compatibility and deepen connections.

Major Planet Alignments
Conjunctions:

- **Astrological Significance:** Conjunctions occur when two or more planets align closely in the same zodiac sign, intensifying their combined energy. This alignment creates a potent blend of the planets' influences, leading to heightened focus and intensity in specific areas of life.
- **Impact on Relationships:** Conjunctions can bring intense attraction and deep connections, but they can also create power struggles and conflicts. The combined energy can amplify both positive and negative traits in a relationship.

Oppositions:

- **Astrological Significance:** Oppositions occur when planets are directly opposite each other in the zodiac, creating a dynamic tension. This alignment highlights contrasts and opposing forces, prompting growth and balance.
- **Impact on Relationships:** Oppositions can create attraction based on differences, fostering growth and understanding. However, they can also lead to conflicts and misunderstandings if not managed carefully.

Trines:

- **Astrological Significance:** Trines occur when planets are 120 degrees apart, creating a harmonious flow of energy. This alignment promotes ease, cooperation, and natural compatibility.
- **Impact on Relationships:** Trines enhance harmony and understanding in relationships, making it easier to connect and communicate. This alignment fosters a sense of ease and natural compatibility between partners.

Squares:

- **Astrological Significance:** Squares occur when planets are 90 degrees apart, creating tension and challenges. This alignment forces growth and change through conflict and resolution.
- **Impact on Relationships:** Squares can create challenges and conflicts in relationships, prompting growth and transformation. While they can be difficult, they also offer opportunities for overcoming obstacles and deepening connections.

Sextiles:

- **Astrological Significance:** Sextiles occur when planets are 60 degrees apart, creating opportunities for cooperation and mutual support. This alignment fosters growth and development through positive interactions.
- **Impact on Relationships:** Sextiles enhance communication and cooperation, making it easier to work together and support each other's growth. This alignment promotes mutual understanding and shared goals.

How to Use Kinks to Enhance Compatibility and Connection During These Alignments

Understanding how to harness the energy of planetary alignments can help you enhance compatibility and deepen your connection with your partner. By incorporating specific kinks and practices that align with the energy of each alignment, you can navigate challenges and maximize the positive aspects of your relationship.

Conjunctions: Harnessing Intensity

Recommended Kinks:

1. **Role-Playing:** Use role-playing to explore intense dynamics and deepen your connection. Conjunctions amplify energy, making it a perfect time to dive into passionate and immersive scenarios.
2. **Impact Play:** Engage in impact play to channel the heightened energy and intensity. Activities like spanking, flogging, or paddling can provide a cathartic release and enhance intimacy.

Practices:

1. **Open Communication:** Ensure clear and open communication to manage the intense energy and avoid misunderstandings.

2. **Balancing Power:** Use kinks that explore power dynamics, balancing control and submission to navigate the intensity of conjunctions.

Oppositions: Embracing Differences
Recommended Kinks:

1. **Sensory Play:** Use sensory play to explore contrasts and opposing sensations. Activities like temperature play (ice and heat) or using different textures can enhance the dynamic tension.
2. **Bondage and Release:** Explore bondage and release dynamics to navigate the push-pull energy of oppositions. This can foster trust and understanding between partners.

Practices:

1. **Compromise and Balance:** Focus on finding balance and compromise in your sexual practices, embracing differences to enhance your connection.
2. **Emotional Exploration:** Use kinks that allow for emotional exploration and vulnerability, helping to bridge gaps and foster deeper understanding.

Trines: Enhancing Harmony
Recommended Kinks:

1. **Sensual Massage:** Use sensual massage to enhance the harmonious energy of trines. This promotes relaxation, connection, and mutual pleasure.
2. **Mutual Masturbation:** Engage in mutual masturbation to explore mutual pleasure and understanding, fostering a deeper connection.

Practices:

1. **Collaborative Exploration:** Use the harmonious energy to explore new kinks and fantasies together, enhancing your sexual connection.
2. **Emotional Intimacy:** Focus on emotional intimacy and open communication, using the ease of trines to deepen your bond.

Squares: Overcoming Challenges
Recommended Kinks:

1. **Power Play:** Use power play dynamics to navigate the tension and challenges of squares. Exploring dominance and submission can help manage conflicts and enhance intimacy.
2. **Cathartic Release:** Engage in activities that provide a cathartic release, such as impact play or primal play, to channel and release built-up tension.

Practices:

1. **Problem-Solving:** Use the challenging energy of squares to address and resolve conflicts in your relationship, enhancing understanding and growth.
2. **Trust-Building Activities:** Focus on trust-building activities that foster communication and mutual support, helping to navigate challenges together.

Sextiles: Fostering Cooperation
Recommended Kinks:

1. **Erotic Communication:** Use erotic communication, such as dirty talk or sharing fantasies, to enhance cooperation and mutual understanding.

2. **Light Bondage:** Engage in light bondage practices that promote trust and cooperation, fostering a sense of mutual support and connection.

Practices:

1. **Exploring New Kinks:** Use the cooperative energy of sextiles to explore new kinks and activities together, enhancing your sexual repertoire.
2. **Mutual Support:** Focus on mutual support and encouragement, using sexual practices that promote shared goals and understanding.

Sample Practices for Planet Alignments
Conjunctions: Passionate Role-Playing Scenario
Materials Needed:

- Costumes or props for role-playing
- Comfortable space

Steps:

1. **Set the Scene:** Choose a passionate and intense role-playing scenario, such as a forbidden romance or a power dynamic.
2. **Discuss Boundaries:** Communicate boundaries and desires before starting.
3. **Immerse in Roles:** Fully immerse in your roles, using the intensified energy of the conjunction to deepen your connection.
4. **Aftercare:** Provide aftercare to ensure both partners feel supported and connected after the intense experience.

Oppositions: Sensory Play Exploration
Materials Needed:

- Ice cubes and warm towels
- Various textured objects (feathers, silk, leather)

Steps:

1. **Create a Comfortable Space:** Set up a comfortable space with all necessary materials.
2. **Discuss Sensations:** Discuss which sensations you both want to explore.
3. **Alternate Sensations:** Alternate between cold and warm sensations, soft and rough textures, to explore contrasts.
4. **Check-In:** Regularly check in with each other to ensure comfort and consent.

Trines: Sensual Massage and Mutual Masturbation
Materials Needed:

- Massage oils
- Soft music and candles

Steps:

1. **Set the Mood:** Create a relaxing atmosphere with soft music and candles.
2. **Massage Each Other:** Take turns giving each other a sensual massage, focusing on relaxation and connection.
3. **Mutual Masturbation:** Transition into mutual masturbation, exploring each other's pleasure and deepening your connection.

Squares: Power Play Dynamics
Materials Needed:

- Restraints (handcuffs, ropes)
- Impact play tools (paddle, flogger)

Steps:

1. **Discuss Boundaries:** Communicate boundaries and safe words before starting.
2. **Explore Power Dynamics:** Engage in power play, exploring dominance and submission.
3. **Provide Aftercare:** After the session, provide aftercare to ensure both partners feel supported and connected.

Sextiles: Erotic Communication and Light Bondage
Materials Needed:

- Soft scarves or silk ties

Steps:

1. **Set the Scene:** Create a comfortable space for open communication.
2. **Share Fantasies:** Take turns sharing erotic fantasies and desires.
3. **Light Bondage:** Incorporate light bondage using soft scarves or silk ties to enhance trust and cooperation.
4. **Check-In:** Regularly check in with each other to ensure comfort and consent.

By understanding the astrological significance of planetary alignments and their impact on relationships and sexuality, you can enhance compatibility and deepen your connection with your partner. Use the energy of these alignments to explore new kinks, address challenges, and foster mutual understanding and growth in your sexual relationship.

Chapter 24: The Wiccan Wheel of the Year - Seasonal Sexual Energy

Overview of the Wiccan Wheel of the Year and Its Eight Sabbats

The Wiccan Wheel of the Year is a calendar of seasonal festivals, known as Sabbats, which celebrate the natural cycles of the Earth and the changing seasons. There are eight Sabbats in the Wheel of the Year, each marking significant points in the solar calendar and reflecting the agricultural and pastoral rhythms of ancient societies. These Sabbats are opportunities for reflection, celebration, and connection with the natural world, and they offer unique energies that can be harnessed to enhance sexual experiences and relationships.

The Eight Sabbats

1. **Samhain (October 31st - November 1st)**
    - **Overview:** Samhain marks the end of the harvest season and the beginning of winter. It is a time to honor ancestors and reflect on mortality and the cycle of life and death.
    - **Energy:** Reflective, transformative, introspective.
2. **Yule (Winter Solstice, around December 21st)**
    - **Overview:** Yule celebrates the winter solstice, the longest night of the year. It marks the rebirth of the Sun and the return of light.
    - **Energy:** Rebirth, renewal, hope.
3. **Imbolc (February 1st - 2nd)**
    - **Overview:** Imbolc marks the midpoint between winter and spring. It is a time of purification and preparation for the coming growth.

- **Energy:** Purification, preparation, anticipation.

4. **Ostara (Spring Equinox, around March 21st)**
   - **Overview:** Ostara celebrates the spring equinox, a time of balance between light and dark. It marks the beginning of spring and new growth.
   - **Energy:** Renewal, balance, fertility.

5. **Beltane (April 30th - May 1st)**
   - **Overview:** Beltane marks the beginning of the summer season and is a celebration of fertility, passion, and the blossoming of life.
   - **Energy:** Passion, fertility, celebration.

6. **Litha (Summer Solstice, around June 21st)**
   - **Overview:** Litha celebrates the summer solstice, the longest day of the year. It is a time of peak energy, abundance, and joy.
   - **Energy:** Abundance, joy, celebration.

7. **Lammas (August 1st)**
   - **Overview:** Lammas, or Lughnasadh, marks the beginning of the harvest season. It is a time to give thanks for the abundance of the Earth.
   - **Energy:** Gratitude, abundance, fulfillment.

8. **Mabon (Autumn Equinox, around September 21st)**
   - **Overview:** Mabon celebrates the autumn equinox, a time of balance between light and dark. It is a time of reflection and gratitude for the harvest.
   - **Energy:** Balance, reflection, gratitude.

Recommended Kinks and Practices for Each Sabbat
Samhain
Recommended Kinks:

1. **Shadow Play:** Explore fantasies and desires that delve into the darker aspects of sexuality, such as role-playing scenarios involving power and control.
2. **Sensory Deprivation:** Use blindfolds and earplugs to heighten other senses and create an introspective experience.

Practices:

1. **Ancestral Connection:** Incorporate rituals that honor ancestors and reflect on the cycle of life and death. Share stories and memories with your partner to deepen your connection.
2. **Transformative Rituals:** Engage in rituals that symbolize transformation and letting go of past inhibitions or negative experiences.

Yule
Recommended Kinks:

1. **Candle Play:** Use candles to explore temperature play, symbolizing the return of light and warmth.
2. **Gift Exchange:** Incorporate a playful gift exchange of erotic items to celebrate the spirit of giving.

Practices:

1. **Rebirth Rituals:** Create a ritual that symbolizes rebirth and renewal, such as a cleansing bath or meditation.
2. **Shared Wishes:** Share your hopes and desires for the coming year with your partner, setting intentions together.

Imbolc

Recommended Kinks:

1. **Purification Play:** Explore kinks that involve purification and cleansing, such as erotic baths or massage with essential oils.
2. **Light Bondage:** Use soft restraints to symbolize preparation and anticipation.

Practices:

1. **Cleansing Rituals:** Perform a cleansing ritual to purify your space and energy, preparing for new growth.
2. **Setting Intentions:** Set intentions for the coming season, focusing on what you wish to cultivate in your relationship.

Ostara

Recommended Kinks:

1. **Fertility Rituals:** Engage in role-playing scenarios that celebrate fertility and new beginnings.
2. **Outdoor Play:** Explore sexual activities in nature to connect with the energy of renewal and growth.

Practices:

1. **Balance Rituals:** Create rituals that symbolize balance, such as meditative practices or yoga together.
2. **Planting Seeds:** Plant seeds together as a symbolic act of setting intentions for growth and new beginnings.

Beltane
Recommended Kinks:

1. **Passion Play:** Explore kinks that celebrate passion and fertility, such as erotic dance or mutual masturbation.
2. **Fire Play:** Use candles or a controlled fire to symbolize the fiery energy of Beltane.

Practices:

1. **Maypole Dance:** Create a ritual dance around a symbolic maypole, celebrating the energy of life and fertility.
2. **Sex Magic:** Practice sex magic by focusing on your shared intentions and desires during lovemaking.

Litha
Recommended Kinks:

1. **Sun Worship:** Incorporate elements of sun worship into your sexual play, such as outdoor activities or positions that honor the Sun.
2. **Sensory Overload:** Use multiple sensory stimuli to celebrate the peak energy and abundance of Litha.

Practices:

1. **Abundance Rituals:** Perform rituals that celebrate abundance and joy, such as a shared feast or a gratitude practice.
2. **Celebration of Light:** Create a ritual that celebrates the longest day of the year, such as watching the sunrise or sunset together.

Lammas
Recommended Kinks:

1. **Harvest Play:** Explore kinks that symbolize the harvest, such as role-playing scenarios involving abundance and fulfillment.
2. **Food Play:** Incorporate food into your sexual play to celebrate the abundance of the Earth.

Practices:

1. **Gratitude Rituals:** Perform rituals that express gratitude for the abundance in your life and relationship.
2. **Harvest Offering:** Create an offering of thanks, such as baking bread together and sharing it with loved ones.

Mabon
Recommended Kinks:

1. **Balance Play:** Explore kinks that symbolize balance and harmony, such as mutual pleasure or synchronized activities.
2. **Sensual Touch:** Focus on sensual touch and massage to enhance connection and gratitude.

Practices:

1. **Reflection Rituals:** Perform rituals that encourage reflection and gratitude for the past season's growth and experiences.
2. **Balance Ceremony:** Create a ceremony that celebrates balance, such as lighting candles or creating an altar that represents both light and dark.

<u>Sample Rituals for Each Sabbat</u>
Samhain: Shadow Play and Ancestral Connection
Materials Needed:

- Black candles
- Blindfolds and earplugs
- Photos or mementos of ancestors

Steps:

1. **Set the Scene:** Create a dimly lit space with black candles and photos or mementos of ancestors.
2. **Discuss Boundaries:** Communicate boundaries and desires before starting shadow play.
3. **Engage in Shadow Play:** Use blindfolds and earplugs to heighten other senses and explore power dynamics.
4. **Honor Ancestors:** After the play, take time to honor your ancestors, sharing stories and memories with your partner.

Yule: Candle Play and Rebirth Rituals
Materials Needed:

- Red and green candles
- Massage oils
- Small gifts for exchange

Steps:

1. **Set the Scene:** Decorate your space with red and green candles, and have massage oils and gifts ready.
2. **Candle Play:** Use candles to explore temperature play, symbolizing the return of light and warmth.

3. **Gift Exchange:** Exchange small erotic gifts to celebrate the spirit of giving.
4. **Rebirth Ritual:** End with a cleansing massage or bath, symbolizing rebirth and renewal.

Imbolc: Purification Play and Cleansing Rituals
Materials Needed:

- White candles
- Essential oils
- Soft restraints

Steps:

1. **Set the Scene:** Create a peaceful space with white candles and essential oils.
2. **Purification Play:** Engage in purification play, such as erotic baths or massages with essential oils.
3. **Light Bondage:** Use soft restraints to symbolize preparation and anticipation.
4. **Cleansing Ritual:** Perform a cleansing ritual to purify your space and energy, preparing for new growth.

Ostara: Fertility Rituals and Planting Seeds
Materials Needed:

- Green candles
- Flower petals
- Seeds and soil

Steps:

1. **Set the Scene:** Decorate your space with green candles and flower petals.
2. **Fertility Rituals:** Engage in role-playing scenarios that celebrate fertility and new beginnings.
3. **Outdoor Play:** Explore sexual activities in nature to connect with the energy of renewal and growth.
4. **Planting Seeds:** End by planting seeds together as a symbolic act of setting intentions for growth and new beginnings

Beltane: Passion Play and Fire Rituals
Materials Needed:

- Red and white candles
- Erotic dance music
- Maypole or symbolic pole

Steps:

1. **Set the Scene:** Decorate your space with red and white candles and set up a maypole or symbolic pole.
2. **Passion Play:** Engage in passionate activities like erotic dance or mutual masturbation.
3. **Fire Ritual:** Use candles or a small fire to symbolize the fiery energy of Beltane. Safely explore temperature play or simply enjoy the warmth and light together.
4. **Maypole Dance:** Create a ritual dance around the maypole, celebrating life, fertility, and passion.

Litha: Sun Worship and Sensory Overload
Materials Needed:

- Yellow and gold candles
- Various sensory items (feathers, ice, warming oils)
- Outdoor space (optional)

Steps:

1. **Set the Scene:** Decorate your space with yellow and gold candles. If possible, create an outdoor setting.
2. **Sun Worship:** Begin with a ritual to honor the Sun, such as watching the sunrise or sunset together.
3. **Sensory Overload:** Use multiple sensory stimuli like feathers, ice, and warming oils to celebrate the peak energy and abundance of Litha.
4. **Celebrate Abundance:** Share a meal or perform a ritual that celebrates the abundance and joy of the season.

Lammas: Harvest Play and Gratitude Rituals
Materials Needed:

- Orange and brown candles
- Fresh bread or baked goods
- Seasonal fruits and vegetables

Steps:

1. **Set the Scene:** Decorate your space with orange and brown candles and have fresh bread or baked goods ready.
2. **Harvest Play:** Engage in role-playing scenarios that celebrate abundance and fulfillment.

3. **Food Play:** Incorporate food into your sexual play to celebrate the Earth's abundance.
4. **Gratitude Ritual:** Perform a ritual that expresses gratitude for the abundance in your life and relationship. Share the fresh bread and seasonal fruits and vegetables as an offering of thanks.

Mabon: Balance Play and Reflection Rituals
Materials Needed:

- Red and brown candles
- Seasonal decorations (leaves, pumpkins)
- Comfortable seating for reflection

Steps:

1. **Set the Scene:** Decorate your space with red and brown candles and seasonal decorations like leaves and pumpkins.
2. **Balance Play:** Explore activities that symbolize balance and harmony, such as mutual pleasure or synchronized movements.
3. **Sensual Touch:** Focus on sensual touch and massage to enhance connection and gratitude.
4. **Reflection Ritual:** Create a ritual that encourages reflection and gratitude for the past season's growth and experiences. Use comfortable seating for a reflective conversation or meditation together.

By aligning your sexual practices with the energies of the Wiccan Wheel of the Year, you can deepen your connection to the natural world and each other. These rituals and kinks can help you harness the seasonal energies to enhance your intimacy, celebrate life's cycles, and set intentions for growth and renewal.

Chapter 25: Integrating Astrology, Cosmic Events, and the Wiccan Wheel

Tips for Combining Astrological Insights, Cosmic Events, Moon Phases, Planetary Alignments, and the Wiccan Wheel of the Year in Your Sexual Practices

Integrating various astrological insights, cosmic events, moon phases, planetary alignments, and the Wiccan Wheel of the Year can enhance your sexual practices by aligning them with the natural rhythms of the cosmos. This holistic approach allows you to deepen your connection with your partner, the universe, and yourself. Here are some tips for combining these elements into your sexual practices:

1. Understand Each Element's Influence

Astrological Insights:

- Recognize the characteristics and sexual traits associated with each zodiac sign.
- Use your astrological birth chart to understand your and your partner's sexual preferences and compatibility.

Cosmic Events:

- Be aware of significant cosmic events like eclipses, retrogrades, and meteor showers.
- Understand how these events influence emotions, energy levels, and relationships.

Moon Phases:

- Align your sexual practices with the moon phases to harness their specific energies (e.g., new beginnings during the New Moon, peak passion during the Full Moon).

Planetary Alignments:

- Identify major planetary alignments and their impact on relationships and sexuality.
- Use these alignments to enhance compatibility and deepen connections.

Wiccan Wheel of the Year:

- Celebrate the eight Sabbats and their seasonal energies.
- Integrate rituals and practices that align with the themes of each Sabbat.

2. Create Themed Rituals and Practices
New Moon:

- Set new sexual intentions and explore new kinks.
- Engage in cleansing rituals to prepare for new beginnings.

Full Moon:

- Indulge in passionate and intense sexual experiences.
- Celebrate the culmination of your efforts and achievements in your relationship.

Solar and Lunar Eclipses:

- Use the transformative energy of eclipses to explore deeper emotional and physical connections.
- Release old patterns and embrace new dynamics in your sexual relationship.

Retrogrades:

- Reflect on past sexual experiences and relationships.
- Improve communication and revisit unresolved issues.

Sabbats:

- Incorporate seasonal themes into your sexual practices (e.g., fertility and passion during Beltane, gratitude and fulfillment during Lammas).
- Celebrate each Sabbat with specific rituals and activities that enhance your connection to the natural world.

3. Use Tools and Props to Enhance Your Practices

- **Candles and Incense:** Use candles and incense to create a magical and sensual atmosphere. Choose colors and scents that align with the astrological or seasonal theme.
- **Crystals and Gemstones:** Incorporate crystals that resonate with specific energies (e.g., rose quartz for love, amethyst for spiritual connection).
- **Essential Oils:** Use essential oils for massages and baths to enhance relaxation and arousal.
- **Tarot Cards and Runes:** Use divination tools to gain insights and set intentions for your sexual practices.

4. Journal and Reflect

- Keep a journal to document your experiences, insights, and intentions.
- Reflect on how integrating these elements impacts your sexual relationship and personal growth.
- Use your journal to track cosmic events, moon phases, and Sabbats, noting any correlations with your sexual experiences.

5. Communicate and Plan with Your Partner

- Discuss your interests and intentions with your partner.
- Plan rituals and activities together, ensuring mutual consent and enthusiasm.
- Use astrological insights and cosmic events as conversation starters to deepen your emotional connection.

Creating a Personalized Sexual Kink Astrology Calendar

Creating a personalized sexual kink astrology calendar allows you to plan and align your sexual practices with cosmic events, moon phases, planetary alignments, and the Wiccan Wheel of the Year. Here's how to create your calendar:

Step 1: Gather Key Dates and Information

1. **Astrological Dates:**
   - Birthdates of you and your partner to identify key zodiac signs and astrological insights.
   - Important transits and alignments (e.g., Venus and Mars transits, Mercury retrograde).
2. **Cosmic Events:**
   - Dates of solar and lunar eclipses, meteor showers, and other significant cosmic events.
3. **Moon Phases:**

- Dates of the New Moon, Full Moon, and other moon phases.

4. **Wiccan Sabbats:**
   - Dates of the eight Sabbats (Samhain, Yule, Imbolc, Ostara, Beltane, Litha, Lammas, Mabon).

Step 2: Create a Calendar Template

1. **Monthly Layout:**
   - Use a calendar template with monthly layouts.
   - Mark the dates of key astrological events, moon phases, and Sabbats.

2. **Sections for Notes:**
   - Include sections for notes, intentions, and reflections for each month.
   - Use these sections to document your experiences and insights.

Step 3: Plan Themed Activities and Rituals

1. **Align Activities with Key Dates:**
   - Plan specific sexual activities, kinks, and rituals that align with the energy of each key date.
   - For example, schedule a passionate role-playing session during the Full Moon or a cleansing ritual during the New Moon.

2. **Incorporate Seasonal Themes:**
   - Integrate themes from the Wiccan Wheel of the Year into your practices.
   - For example, celebrate Beltane with fertility rituals and Lammas with gratitude practices.

Step 4: Communicate and Collaborate

1. **Discuss Plans with Your Partner:**
    - Share your calendar and planned activities with your partner.
    - Ensure mutual consent and enthusiasm for each activity and ritual.
2. **Set Intentions Together:**
    - Use the calendar to set shared intentions and goals for your sexual relationship.
    - Reflect on these intentions regularly and adjust your plans as needed.

Step 5: Reflect and Adjust

1. **Keep a Journal:**
    - Document your experiences, insights, and reflections in a journal.
    - Note how each cosmic event, moon phase, or Sabbat impacts your sexual relationship.
2. **Review and Adjust:**
    - Regularly review your calendar and journal entries.
    - Adjust your plans based on your experiences and evolving desires.

Sample Calendar Entry
January:

- **New Moon (January 6th):**
    - Activity: Set new sexual intentions with your partner.
    - Ritual: Perform a cleansing bath together to prepare for new beginnings.
    - Notes: Reflect on what you wish to explore and achieve in your sexual relationship this month.
- **Full Moon (January 20th):**

- ◦ Activity: Plan a passionate and intense sexual experience.
- ◦ Ritual: Light candles and use essential oils to create a sensual atmosphere.
- ◦ Notes: Celebrate your connection and the culmination of your efforts.
- **Imbolc (February 1st):**
  - ◦ Activity: Engage in purification play, such as erotic baths or massages with essential oils.
  - ◦ Ritual: Perform a cleansing ritual to purify your space and energy.
  - ◦ Notes: Set intentions for the coming season and prepare for new growth.

By integrating astrological insights, cosmic events, moon phases, planetary alignments, and the Wiccan Wheel of the Year into your sexual practices, you can create a rich and meaningful sexual relationship that aligns with the natural rhythms of the cosmos. Use your personalized sexual kink astrology calendar to plan and document your journey, enhancing your connection with your partner and the universe.

Chapter 26: Embracing Your Cosmic Kinks
Summary of Key Points

In the journey through this book, you've explored the profound connections between astrology, cosmic events, moon phases, planetary alignments, and the Wiccan Wheel of the Year and their influences on sexuality and kinks. Let's summarize the key points covered:

Astrological Insights and Sexuality

- **Zodiac Signs:** Understanding the sexual characteristics and kinks associated with each zodiac sign can deepen your self-awareness and enhance your relationships.
- **Birth Charts:** Your astrological birth chart offers insights into your sexual preferences, desires, and compatibility with others.

Cosmic Events

- **Solar and Lunar Eclipses:** These events bring powerful shifts and opportunities for transformation, making them ideal times for exploring deep emotional connections and new sexual dynamics.
- **Retrogrades:** Periods of reflection and reassessment, retrogrades encourage resolving past issues and improving communication in relationships.
- **Meteor Showers:** These events inspire magic and inspiration, perfect for exploring romantic fantasies and outdoor sexual activities.

Moon Phases

- **New Moon:** A time for new beginnings and setting intentions, the New Moon is ideal for exploring new kinks and cleansing rituals.
- **Full Moon:** Heightened emotions and peak energy make the Full Moon perfect for passionate and intense sexual experiences.
- **Waning Phases:** Reflective and introspective, these phases encourage letting go of negativity and nurturing connections.

Planetary Alignments

- **Conjunctions:** Intensify relationships and create deep connections, making them ideal for role-playing and impact play.
- **Oppositions:** Highlight contrasts and opposing forces, encouraging exploration of sensory play and emotional bondage.
- **Trines and Sextiles:** Foster harmony and cooperation, enhancing mutual pleasure and communication.

Wiccan Wheel of the Year

- **Eight Sabbats:** Celebrating the natural cycles of the Earth, each Sabbat offers unique energies to incorporate into your sexual practices, from passion and fertility at Beltane to reflection and gratitude at Mabon.

Final Thoughts on Exploring and Embracing Your Cosmic Sexuality and Kinks

Embracing Your Cosmic Sexuality

Exploring your cosmic sexuality involves understanding and aligning your sexual practices with the natural rhythms and energies of the cosmos. By integrating astrological insights, cosmic events, moon phases, planetary alignments, and the Wiccan Wheel of the Year into your sexual journey, you can achieve a deeper connection with yourself, your partner, and the universe. This holistic approach not only enhances your sexual experiences but also promotes personal growth, emotional intimacy, and spiritual fulfillment.

Key Takeaways

1. **Self-Awareness:** Understanding your astrological influences can provide valuable insights into your sexual preferences and desires, fostering self-awareness and acceptance.
2. **Connection:** Aligning your sexual practices with cosmic events and natural cycles can deepen your connection with your partner, creating a more harmonious and fulfilling relationship.
3. **Growth:** Embracing the energies of the cosmos encourages personal and relational growth, helping you overcome challenges and explore new dimensions of your sexuality.
4. **Balance:** Integrating the phases of the moon and the Wiccan Sabbats into your sexual practices promotes balance, reflection, and renewal, enhancing your overall well-being.

Encouragement to Keep Discovering and Enjoying Your Kinky Journey

Your journey into cosmic sexuality and kinks is a continuous and evolving process. Here are some final thoughts to encourage you to keep discovering and enjoying your kinky journey:

1. **Stay Curious:** Keep exploring new aspects of your sexuality and remain open to discovering new kinks and practices. The cosmos is vast, and there is always more to learn and experience.
2. **Communicate:** Maintain open and honest communication with your partner. Share your discoveries, desires, and boundaries to foster mutual understanding and deepen your connection.

3. **Reflect and Adjust:** Regularly reflect on your experiences and adjust your practices based on what you learn. Use your journal to document insights and track your growth.
4. **Celebrate:** Celebrate your journey and the milestones you achieve. Whether it's a successful new ritual, a deepened connection, or a personal breakthrough, take time to acknowledge and appreciate your progress.
5. **Honor the Natural Cycles:** Embrace the natural cycles of the cosmos and align your practices with these rhythms. Doing so enhances your connection to the universe and promotes a sense of harmony and balance.
6. **Prioritize Consent and Safety:** Always prioritize consent and safety in your sexual practices. Ensure that both you and your partner feel comfortable and respected in every exploration.

Final Words

Embracing your cosmic kinks and sexuality is a powerful journey of self-discovery, connection, and growth. By aligning your sexual practices with the energies of the cosmos, you can create a more fulfilling and harmonious sexual relationship. Remember, this journey is uniquely yours—honor it, nurture it, and continue to explore the boundless possibilities that lie ahead.

May the stars guide you, the moon inspire you, and the natural cycles of the Earth ground you in your journey of cosmic sexuality. Keep exploring, stay curious, and enjoy every moment of your kinky adventure. The universe is your playground—embrace it with passion, creativity, and an open heart.

<u>Appendix</u>
Glossary of Astrological and Kink Terms
Astrological Terms
Zodiac Signs
Aries (March 21 - April 19):

- **Characteristics:** Bold, energetic, adventurous, and assertive.
- **Sexual Traits:** Passionate, dominant, and enjoys taking the lead.

Taurus (April 20 - May 20):

- **Characteristics:** Sensual, patient, reliable, and determined.
- **Sexual Traits:** Sensual, enjoys prolonged foreplay, and values physical touch.

Gemini (May 21 - June 20):

- **Characteristics:** Versatile, communicative, curious, and intellectual.
- **Sexual Traits:** Experimental, enjoys variety, and mentally stimulating encounters.

Cancer (June 21 - July 22):

- **Characteristics:** Nurturing, empathetic, intuitive, and protective.
- **Sexual Traits:** Emotionally connected, enjoys intimacy and security in sexual relationships.

Leo (July 23 - August 22):

- **Characteristics:** Confident, charismatic, creative, and generous.
- **Sexual Traits:** Theatrical, enjoys being adored, and passionate.

Virgo (August 23 - September 22):

- **Characteristics:** Analytical, practical, detail-oriented, and modest.
- **Sexual Traits:** Precise, enjoys service-oriented roles, and values cleanliness.

Libra (September 23 - October 22):

- **Characteristics:** Balanced, social, diplomatic, and romantic.
- **Sexual Traits:** Romantic, enjoys harmony, and aesthetically pleasing environments.

Scorpio (October 23 - November 21):

- **Characteristics:** Intense, passionate, secretive, and resourceful.
- **Sexual Traits:** Deeply passionate, enjoys power dynamics, and intense connections.

Sagittarius (November 22 - December 21):

- **Characteristics:** Adventurous, optimistic, independent, and philosophical.

- **Sexual Traits:** Free-spirited, enjoys exploration and novelty, and prefers non-committal encounters.

Capricorn (December 22 - January 19):

- **Characteristics:** Disciplined, ambitious, practical, and responsible.
- **Sexual Traits:** Traditional, enjoys control and structure, and prefers reliability.

Aquarius (January 20 - February 18):

- **Characteristics:** Innovative, independent, humanitarian, and intellectual.
- **Sexual Traits:** Experimental, enjoys unconventional practices, and values intellectual connection.

Pisces (February 19 - March 20):

- **Characteristics:** Dreamy, empathetic, artistic, and compassionate.
- **Sexual Traits:** Romantic, enjoys emotional and spiritual connections, and imaginative.

Moon Phases
New Moon:

- **Description:** The beginning of the lunar cycle, when the moon is not visible from Earth.
- **Energy:** New beginnings, setting intentions, and cleansing.
- **Sexual Influence:** Ideal time for exploring new kinks and setting sexual intentions.

Waxing Crescent:

- **Description:** The moon starts to become visible, growing in light.
- **Energy:** Building momentum, planning, and anticipation.
- **Sexual Influence:** Perfect for building sexual tension and exploring new possibilities.

First Quarter:

- **Description:** Half of the moon is visible, representing action and decision-making.
- **Energy:** Taking initiative, overcoming challenges, and progress.
- **Sexual Influence:** Great for taking action in sexual desires and exploring new dynamics.

Waxing Gibbous:

- **Description:** The moon is nearly full, representing refinement and focus.
- **Energy:** Refining efforts, preparing for culmination, and attention to detail.
- **Sexual Influence:** Time for fine-tuning sexual practices and deepening intimacy.

Full Moon:

- **Description:** The moon is fully illuminated.
- **Energy:** Peak energy, heightened emotions, and culmination.
- **Sexual Influence:** Ideal for passionate and intense sexual experiences.

Waning Gibbous:

- **Description:** The moon starts to decrease in light, representing gratitude and sharing.
- **Energy:** Reflection, sharing, and gratitude.
- **Sexual Influence:** Perfect for nurturing connections and mutual pleasure.

Last Quarter:

- **Description:** Half of the moon is visible, representing reflection and release.
- **Energy:** Letting go, reassessment, and adjustments.
- **Sexual Influence:** Ideal for emotional release and letting go of past sexual inhibitions.

Waning Crescent:

- **Description:** The final phase before the New Moon, representing rest and preparation.
- **Energy:** Rest, recuperation, and preparation.
- **Sexual Influence:** Perfect for gentle, nurturing sexual practices and setting the stage for new beginnings.

Planetary Alignments
Conjunction:

- **Description:** When two or more planets align closely in the same zodiac sign.
- **Energy:** Intensified focus and energy, bringing combined planetary influences.

- **Sexual Influence:** Ideal for deep connections and exploring intense sexual dynamics.

Opposition:

- **Description:** When planets are directly opposite each other in the zodiac.
- **Energy:** Dynamic tension, highlighting contrasts and balance.
- **Sexual Influence:** Great for exploring contrasts and balancing power dynamics.

Trine:

- **Description:** When planets are 120 degrees apart, creating a harmonious flow of energy.
- **Energy:** Ease, cooperation, and natural compatibility.
- **Sexual Influence:** Enhances harmony and mutual understanding in sexual relationships.

Square:

- **Description:** When planets are 90 degrees apart, creating tension and challenges.
- **Energy:** Conflict, growth through challenges, and resolution.
- **Sexual Influence:** Ideal for addressing and overcoming sexual challenges, fostering growth.

Sextile:

- **Description:** When planets are 60 degrees apart, creating opportunities for cooperation.
- **Energy:** Growth, development, and positive interactions.

- **Sexual Influence:** Enhances communication and mutual support in sexual practices.

Wiccan Sabbats
Samhain:

- **Description:** Celebrated on October 31st - November 1st, marking the end of the harvest season.
- **Energy:** Reflective, transformative, and introspective.
- **Sexual Influence:** Ideal for exploring shadow play and honoring ancestors.

Yule:

- **Description:** Celebrated during the Winter Solstice (around December 21st), marking the rebirth of the Sun.
- **Energy:** Rebirth, renewal, and hope.
- **Sexual Influence:** Perfect for candle play and rituals of rebirth.

Imbolc:

- **Description:** Celebrated on February 1st - 2nd, marking the midpoint between winter and spring.
- **Energy:** Purification, preparation, and anticipation.
- **Sexual Influence:** Ideal for purification play and setting new intentions.

Ostara:

- **Description:** Celebrated during the Spring Equinox (around March 21st), marking the beginning of spring.
- **Energy:** Renewal, balance, and fertility.

- **Sexual Influence:** Great for fertility rituals and outdoor sexual activities.

Beltane:

- **Description:** Celebrated on April 30th - May 1st, marking the beginning of summer.
- **Energy:** Passion, fertility, and celebration.
- **Sexual Influence:** Perfect for passion play and fire rituals.

Litha:

- **Description:** Celebrated during the Summer Solstice (around June 21st), marking the longest day of the year.
- **Energy:** Abundance, joy, and celebration.
- **Sexual Influence:** Ideal for sun worship and sensory overload activities.

Lammas:

- **Description:** Celebrated on August 1st, marking the beginning of the harvest season.
- **Energy:** Gratitude, abundance, and fulfillment.
- **Sexual Influence:** Great for harvest play and food-related sexual activities.

Mabon:

- **Description:** Celebrated during the Autumn Equinox (around September 21st), marking a time of balance.
- **Energy:** Balance, reflection, and gratitude.
- **Sexual Influence:** Perfect for balance play and reflection rituals.

Kink Terms
Sensory Play
Temperature Play:

- **Description:** Involves the use of hot and cold stimuli on the body to heighten arousal and sensory experiences.
- **Techniques:**
    - **Hot:** Warm oils, hot wax (commonly known as wax play), heated stones, or warm water.
    - **Cold:** Ice cubes, chilled metal objects, cold water, or refrigerated toys.
- **Safety:**
    - Ensure clear communication and consent before beginning temperature play.
    - Always test temperatures on yourself before applying them to your partner to avoid burns or frostbite.
    - Avoid extreme temperatures that can cause skin damage or discomfort.

Sensory Deprivation:

- **Description:** The removal or limitation of one or more senses to enhance other senses and increase focus on touch, sound, and sensation.
- **Techniques:**
    - **Blindfolds:** Cover the eyes to heighten the sense of touch.
    - **Earplugs or Headphones:** Muffle or eliminate sound to focus on tactile sensations.
    - **Restraints:** Limit movement to heighten anticipation and sensory experience.
- **Safety:**
    - Establish clear communication and safe signals that don't rely on speech.

- Regularly check in with the deprived partner to ensure they are comfortable and consenting.
- Have safe words and gestures agreed upon beforehand.

Bondage and Discipline
Bondage:

- **Description:** The practice of tying, binding, or restraining a partner for erotic, aesthetic, or psychological pleasure.
- **Techniques:**
    - **Ropes:** Use various knots and ties to restrain the body.
    - **Handcuffs:** Metal or soft cuffs that secure wrists or ankles.
    - **Bondage Tape:** Adhesive-free tape that sticks to itself, not the skin.
    - **Shibari:** A Japanese form of rope bondage that focuses on intricate patterns and aesthetic ties.
- **Safety:**
    - Ensure proper circulation by checking for changes in color or temperature of the bound limbs.
    - Have safety scissors nearby to quickly cut ropes if needed.
    - Avoid placing restraints around the neck or other sensitive areas.

Impact Play:

- **Description:** Involves striking the body with hands or implements to create pleasurable sensations.
- **Techniques:**
    - **Spanking:** Using hands, paddles, or crops on the buttocks.
    - **Flogging:** Using a multi-tailed whip, usually made of leather.
    - **Paddling:** Using a flat, often wooden implement to strike the body.

- **Caning:** Using a thin, flexible cane to deliver sharp blows.
- **Safety:**
  - Start with lighter strikes and gradually increase intensity.
  - Avoid hitting sensitive areas such as the spine, kidneys, and joints.
  - Communicate continuously with your partner and respect safe words.

Role-Playing:

- **Description:** Acting out fantasies or scenarios to enhance sexual excitement and explore different identities.
- **Techniques:**
  - **Costumes:** Dress up as characters relevant to the scenario (e.g., doctor/nurse, teacher/student).
  - **Props:** Use items that add realism to the role-play (e.g., stethoscopes, rulers).
  - **Scripts:** Prepare dialogue or scenarios to guide the role-play.
- **Safety:**
  - Discuss boundaries and scenarios beforehand to ensure mutual comfort.
  - Establish safe words to pause or stop the role-play if needed.
  - Ensure that all role-play activities are consensual and respectful of boundaries.

Dominance and Submission
Dominance and Submission (D/s):

- **Description:** A power exchange dynamic where one partner (the Dominant) takes control, and the other (the Submissive) submits to their authority.

- **Techniques:**
    - **Commands:** The Dominant gives orders that the Submissive follows.
    - **Protocols:** Establishing rules and rituals that the Submissive adheres to.
    - **Collaring:** Symbolic of ownership and commitment in a D/s relationship.
- **Safety:**
    - Clear communication of limits, boundaries, and desires.
    - Use of safe words to ensure activities remain consensual.
    - Regular check-ins and aftercare to support the Submissive's well-being.

Service Submission:

- **Description:** A form of submission focused on performing tasks or services for the Dominant's pleasure or convenience.
- **Techniques:**
    - **Domestic Service:** Cleaning, cooking, or organizing.
    - **Personal Service:** Dressing, grooming, or other personal care tasks.
    - **Erotic Service:** Sexual acts performed to please the Dominant.
- **Safety:**
    - Establish clear guidelines and expectations for service tasks.
    - Ensure tasks are within the Submissive's capabilities and comfort zone.
    - Provide positive reinforcement and aftercare.

Sadomasochism (S/M):

- **Description:** The giving (sadism) and receiving (masochism) of pain for sexual pleasure.

- **Techniques:**
    - **Spanking:** Using hands or implements to deliver strikes.
    - **Whipping:** Using whips or floggers to create pain sensations.
    - **Needle Play:** Using needles to create controlled piercings.
- **Safety:**
    - Start with mild sensations and gradually increase intensity.
    - Ensure all tools are sanitized and safe for use.
    - Regularly check in with the partner receiving pain to ensure they are comfortable and consenting.

Fetishes
Foot Fetish:

- **Description:** Sexual arousal centered on feet or footwear.
- **Techniques:**
    - **Foot Worship:** Kissing, licking, or massaging the feet.
    - **Shoe Play:** Using shoes or boots as part of sexual activities.
    - **Trampling:** Walking or standing on the body with bare feet or shoes.
- **Safety:**
    - Ensure hygiene and cleanliness of the feet.
    - Communicate boundaries and comfort levels.
    - Avoid applying too much pressure during trampling to prevent injury.

Leather Fetish:

- **Description:** Sexual attraction to leather clothing or accessories.
- **Techniques:**
    - **Wearing Leather:** Incorporating leather garments into sexual activities.
    - **Leather Bondage:** Using leather restraints and cuffs.

- **Scent Play:** Enjoying the smell of leather as part of the experience.
- **Safety:**
    - Ensure leather gear fits properly and does not restrict circulation.
    - Clean and maintain leather items to prevent skin irritation or infections.
    - Communicate preferences and boundaries with your partner.

Medical Fetish:

- **Description:** Sexual arousal from medical scenarios, equipment, or role-playing.
- **Techniques:**
    - **Examinations:** Role-playing doctor/patient scenarios.
    - **Medical Instruments:** Using items like stethoscopes, syringes (without needles), and speculums.
    - **Uniforms:** Wearing medical attire such as lab coats or nurse outfits.
- **Safety:**
    - Use only clean and sterile equipment.
    - Avoid invasive procedures that can cause harm.
    - Communicate clearly and respect boundaries.

Other Kinks
Voyeurism:

- **Description:** Sexual arousal from watching others engage in sexual activities.
- **Techniques:**
    - **Mutual Voyeurism:** Watching and being watched by your partner.

- **Erotic Viewing:** Watching erotic films or live performances together.
- **Safety:**
  - Ensure all parties involved consent to being watched.
  - Respect privacy and legal boundaries when engaging in voyeurism.

Exhibitionism:

- **Description:** Sexual arousal from displaying oneself sexually to others.
- **Techniques:**
  - **Private Exhibitionism:** Performing sexual acts for a partner's viewing pleasure.
  - **Public Display:** Engaging in discreet sexual acts in semi-public places (within legal limits).
- **Safety:**
  - Ensure all participants consent to being watched.
  - Be aware of legal boundaries and privacy laws.
  - Avoid exposing non-consenting individuals to sexual acts.

Pet Play:

- **Description:** Role-playing where one partner takes on the persona of an animal, and the other acts as the owner.
- **Techniques:**
  - **Costumes and Gear:** Wearing collars, leashes, tails, and ears.
  - **Behavioral Role-Playing:** Engaging in activities like fetch, grooming, and training.
  - **Verbal Commands:** Using commands and praise to enhance the dynamic.
- **Safety:**

- ◦ Establish clear boundaries and safe words.
- ◦ Ensure costumes and gear fit comfortably and do not restrict movement or breathing.
- ◦ Regularly check in with the person in the animal role to ensure their comfort.

Age Play:

- **Description:** Role-playing where participants take on roles of different ages, such as adult/baby or teacher/student.
- **Techniques:**
    - ◦ **Costumes and Props:** Using items like diapers, pacifiers, or school uniforms.
    - ◦ **Behavioral Role-Playing:** Engaging in activities like feeding, story-telling, or homework.
    - ◦ **Verbal Interaction:** Using appropriate language and tone for the chosen roles.
- **Safety:**
    - ◦ Establish clear boundaries and consent for the age roles being played.
    - ◦ Ensure that all activities are consensual and within legal boundaries.
    - ◦ Provide aftercare to support emotional well-being after role-playing sessions.

By understanding these kink terms in detail, you can explore your desires safely and consensually, enhancing your sexual experiences and deepening your connections with your partners. Whether you're curious about trying something new or looking to deepen your current practices, embracing your kinks with knowledge and respect can lead to a more fulfilling and enjoyable sexual

Resources for Further Reading and Exploration

Books on Astrology and Sexuality

"Sexual Astrology: The Astrology of Sex and the Sexes" by Joanna Martine Woolfolk

This book provides an in-depth look at how astrological signs influence sexual compatibility, preferences, and behaviors. It's an excellent resource for anyone looking to understand the sexual characteristics of each zodiac sign and how to enhance intimacy using astrology.

"Astrology for the Soul" by Jan Spiller

While not exclusively focused on sexuality, this book delves into the North Nodes and South Nodes of the Moon, offering insights into karmic paths and personal growth. Understanding these aspects can help deepen your understanding of yourself and your sexual desires.

"The Astrology of Love & Sex: A Modern Compatibility Guide" by Annabel Gat

This comprehensive guide explores astrological compatibility in romantic and sexual relationships. It includes practical advice, detailed descriptions of each sign's sexual traits, and tips for enhancing intimacy based on astrological insights.

"The Only Astrology Book You'll Ever Need" by Joanna Martine Woolfolk

A foundational text for astrology enthusiasts, this book covers everything from sun signs to planetary alignments. It's a great resource for understanding the basics of astrology and how to apply it to various aspects of life, including sexuality.

Books on Kink and BDSM

"The New Topping Book" and "The New Bottoming Book" by Dossie Easton and Janet W. Hardy

These companion books are essential readings for anyone interested in power exchange dynamics. They offer practical advice, personal anecdotes, and a comprehensive look at the roles of Dominant and Submissive.

"SM 101: A Realistic Introduction" by Jay Wiseman

A thorough introduction to BDSM practices, this book covers safety, communication, and techniques. It's a valuable resource for both beginners and experienced practitioners looking to deepen their knowledge.

"The Ultimate Guide to Kink: BDSM, Role Play and the Erotic Edge" edited by Tristan Taormino

This anthology features essays by leading kink educators and practitioners, offering insights into a wide range of BDSM activities and philosophies. It's a great resource for exploring new kinks and understanding the diverse world of BDSM.

"Playing Well with Others: Your Field Guide to Discovering, Exploring and Navigating the Kink, Leather and BDSM Communities" by Lee Harrington and Mollena Williams

This guidebook is perfect for anyone looking to get involved in the kink community. It covers etiquette, community structures, and practical advice for attending events and finding like-minded individuals.

Books on Tantra and Sacred Sexuality

"Urban Tantra: Sacred Sex for the Twenty-First Century" by Barbara Carrellas

This modern guide to Tantra blends traditional practices with contemporary insights. It includes exercises, techniques, and meditations to enhance intimacy and spiritual connection.

"Tantra: The Art of Conscious Loving" by Charles and Caroline Muir

This classic book on Tantra offers a step-by-step guide to incorporating Tantric practices into your relationship. It focuses on communication, connection, and sexual healing.

"The Heart of Tantric Sex: A Unique Guide to Love and Sexual Fulfillment" by Diana Richardson

This book explores the principles of Tantric sex, emphasizing slow, mindful connection and deep emotional intimacy. It's a great resource for couples looking to enhance their sexual and emotional bond.

Websites and Online Communities
FetLife (www.fetlife.com)

FetLife is a social networking site for the BDSM, fetish, and kink communities. It offers a platform for meeting like-minded individuals, discussing kinks, and finding events and groups in your area.

Reddit - r/BDSMcommunity (www.reddit.com/r/BDSMcommunity)

This subreddit is a supportive and informative space for discussing BDSM practices, sharing experiences, and seeking advice. It's a valuable resource for both beginners and experienced practitioners.

Kinkly (www.kinkly.com)

Kinkly offers a wealth of information on various kinks and fetishes, sexual health, and pleasure. It features articles, guides, and a sex dictionary to help you explore and understand different aspects of sexuality.

Astrology.com (www.astrology.com)

Astrology.com provides daily horoscopes, detailed astrological reports, and articles on various astrological topics. It's a great resource for staying informed about cosmic events and their potential impact on your life.

Cafe Astrology (www.cafeastrology.com)

Cafe Astrology offers comprehensive natal charts, compatibility reports, and in-depth articles on astrology. It's a valuable resource for deepening your understanding of astrological influences on your personality and relationships.

Workshops and Events
BDSM Workshops and Classes

Many cities offer workshops and classes on BDSM techniques, safety, and communication. Look for local events at kink clubs, adult stores, or through community organizations like The Eulenspiegel Society (TES) or The Society of Janus.

Tantra Workshops and Retreats

Tantra workshops and retreats are available worldwide and offer immersive experiences to learn and practice Tantric techniques. Look for reputable instructors and organizations, such as Charles and Caroline Muir's Source School of Tantra Yoga.

Astrology Conferences and Seminars

Astrology conferences and seminars provide opportunities to learn from experienced astrologers and connect with other enthusiasts. Events like the United Astrology Conference (UAC) or the International Society for Astrological Research (ISAR) conferences are excellent places to deepen your knowledge.

YouTube Channels and Podcasts
YouTube Channels

- **AstroLada:** Offers detailed astrological forecasts and educational videos on various astrological topics.
- **Sexplanations:** Hosted by Dr. Lindsey Doe, this channel provides informative videos on sexual health, pleasure, and various kinks.

Podcasts

- **Savage Lovecast:** Hosted by Dan Savage, this podcast covers a wide range of topics related to sex, relationships, and kink, offering advice and insights.
- **The Heart:** This podcast explores intimate and sexual experiences, often delving into topics related to kink and non-traditional relationships.
- **Speaking of Sex with The Pleasure Mechanics:** This podcast provides practical advice on sexual health, pleasure, and exploring kinks.

Online Courses and Educational Platforms
Kink Academy (www.kinkacademy.com)

Kink Academy offers a vast library of instructional videos on various kinks and BDSM practices, taught by experienced educators. It's a valuable resource for learning new techniques and enhancing your knowledge.

OMGYes (www.omgyes.com)

OMGYes is an interactive platform focused on female pleasure, offering research-based techniques and tips for enhancing sexual experiences. It's a great resource for couples looking to improve their sexual connection.

Astrology University (www.astrologyuniversity.com)

Astrology University offers online courses, webinars, and workshops on various astrological topics. It's an excellent resource for deepening your astrological knowledge and applying it to different aspects of life, including sexuality.

Conclusion

Exploring your cosmic kinks and sexuality is a lifelong journey of discovery, growth, and connection. These resources provide a wealth of information and support to help you navigate this journey with confidence and curiosity. Whether you're new to astrology and kink or looking to deepen your existing knowledge, there is always more to learn and explore.

Remember to approach your exploration with an open mind, clear communication, and a focus on mutual consent and respect. Embrace the opportunity to connect with like-minded individuals, seek out new experiences, and continuously evolve in your understanding and practice of cosmic sexuality.

May your journey be filled with passion, enlightenment, and endless possibilities.

Message from the Author:

I hope you enjoyed this book, I love astrology and knew there was not a book such as this out on the shelf. I love metaphysical items as well. Please check out my other books:

-Life of Government Benefits

-My life of Hell

-My life with Hydrocephalus

-Red Sky

-World Domination:Woman's rule

-World Domination:Woman's Rule 2: The War

-Life and Banishment of Apophis: book 1

-The Kidney Friendly Diet

-The Ultimate Hemp Cookbook

-Creating a Dispensary(legally)

-Cleanliness throughout life: the importance of showering from childhood to adulthood.

-Strong Roots: The Risks of Overcoddling children

-Hemp Horoscopes: Cosmic Insights and Earthly Healing

- Celestial Hemp Navigating the Zodiac: Through the Green Cosmos

-Astrological Hemp: Aligning The Stars with Earth's Ancient Herb

-The Astrological Guide to Hemp: Stars, Signs, and Sacred Leaves

-Green Growth: Innovative Marketing Strategies for your Hemp Products and Dispensary

-Cosmic Cannabis

-Astrological Munchies

-Henry The Hemp

-Zodiacal Roots: The Astrological Soul Of Hemp

- **Green Constellations: Intersection of Hemp and Zodiac**

-Hemp in The Houses: An astrological Adventure Through The Cannabis Galaxy

-Galactic Ganja Guide

Heavenly Hemp

Zodiac Leaves

Doctor Who Astrology

Cannastrology

Stellar Satvias and Cosmic Indicas

Celestial Cannabis: A Zodiac Journey

AstroHerbology: The Sky and The Soil: Volume 1

AstroHerbology:Celestial Cannabis:Volume 2

Cosmic Cannabis Cultivation

The Starry Guide to Herbal Harmony: Volume 1

The Starry Guide to Herbal Harmony: Cannabis Universe: Volume 2

Yugioh Astrology: Astrological Guide to Deck, Duels and more

Nightmare Mansion: Echoes of The Abyss

Nightmare Mansion 2: Legacy of Shadows

Nightmare Mansion 3: Shadows of the Forgotten

Nightmare Mansion 4: Echoes of the Damned

The Life and Banishment of Apophis: Book 2

Nightmare Mansion: Halls of Despair

Healing with Herb: Cannabis and Hydrocephalus

Planetary Pot: Aligning with Astrological Herbs: Volume 1

Fast Track to Freedom: 30 Days to Financial Independence Using AI, Assets, and Agile Hustles

Cosmic Hemp Pathways

How to Become Financially Free in 30 Days: 10,000 Paths to Prosperity

Zodiacal Herbage: Astrological Insights: Volume 1

Nightmare Mansion: Whispers in the Walls

The Daleks Invade Atlantis

Henry the hemp and Hydrocephalus

10X The Kidney Friendly Diet

Cannabis Universe: Adult coloring book

Hemp Astrology: The Healing Power of the Stars

Zodiacal Herbage: Astrological Insights: Cannabis Universe: Volume 2

<u>Planetary Pot: Aligning with Astrological Herbs: Cannabis Universes: Volume 2</u>

Doctor Who Meets the Replicators and SG-1: The Ultimate Battle for Survival

Nightmare Mansion: Curse of the Blood Moon

<u>The Celestial Stoner: A Guide to the Zodiac</u>

Cosmic Pleasures: Sex Toy Astrology for Every Sign

Hydrocephalus Astrology: Navigating the Stars and Healing Waters

Lapis and the Mischievous Chocolate Bar

Celestial Positions: Sexual Astrology for Every Sign

Apophis's Shadow Work Journal: : A Journey of Self-Discovery and Healing

Check out my Virtual dispensary for all your hemp needs: https://shift.store/sg1fan23477/retail

If you want solar for your home go here: https://www.harborsolar.live/apophisenterprises/

Get Some Tarot cards: https://www.makeplayingcards.com/sell/apophis-occult-shop

Get some shirts: https://www.bonfire.com/store/apophis-shirt-emporium/

Instagrams:
@apophis_enterprises,
@hempkingdom2024,
@apophisbookemporium,
@apophisscardshop

Twitter: @apophisenterpr1,
Tiktok:@apophisenterprise

Youtube: @sg1fan23477, @FiresideRetreatKingdom

Podcast: Apophis Chat Zone: https://open.spotify.com/show/5zXbrCLEV2xzCp8ybrfHsk?si=fb4d4fdbdce44dec

Newsletter: https://apophiss-newsletter-27c897.beehiiv.com/